MICHAEL
SCHUMACHER

By the same author:

NIGEL MANSELL
The Lion at Bay

AYRTON SENNA

AYRTON SENNA
The Legend Grows

JAMES HUNT
Portrait of a champion

GERHARD BERGER
The human face of Formula 1

AYRTON SENNA
The hard edge of genius

TORVILL AND DEAN
The full story

TWO WHEEL SHOWDOWN!
The full drama of the races which decided
the World 500cc Motor Cycle Championship
from 1949

GRAND PRIX SHOWDOWN!
The full drama of the races which decided
the World Championship 1950–92

HONDA
Conquerors of the track

HONDA
The conquest of Formula 1

NIGEL MANSELL
The making of a champion

ALAIN PROST

Patrick Stephens Limited, an imprint of Haynes Publishing, has published authoritative, quality books for more than a quarter of a century. During that time the company has established a reputation as one of the world's leading publishers of books on aviation, maritime, motor cycle, car, motorsport, and railway subjects. Readers or authors with suggestions for books they would like to see published are invited to write to: The Editorial Director, Patrick Stephens Limited, Sparkford, Nr Yeovil, Somerset BA22 7JJ.

MICHAEL
SCHUMACHER

DEFENDING THE CROWN

Christopher Hilton

Patrick Stephens Limited

First published in December 1994 as
Michael Schumacher: Full Drama of the 1994 World Championship
Second edition (*Defending the Crown*)
published in July 1995

British Library Cataloguing-in-Publication Data:
A catalogue record for this book is
available from the British Library.

ISBN: 1 85260 542 1

Patrick Stephens Limited is an imprint of Haynes Publishing,
Sparkford, Nr. Yeovil, Somerset BA22 7JJ.

Designed & typeset by G&M, Raunds, Northamptonshire.
Printed in Great Britain by Butler & Tanner Ltd, London and Frome.

Contents

Acknowledgements

MY THANKS TO Martin Brundle, Julian Bailey, Alessandro Zanardi, Johnny Herbert, Heinz-Harald Frentzen, Jochen Mass, Eddie Jordan, Dave Price, Albert Hamper, Allan McNish, Otto Rensing, Josef Kaufmann, Peter Hantscher, Wolfgang Schattling of Mercedes, Peter Sieber, Dick Bennetts, Keke Rosberg, Elmar Hoffmann; Gustav Hoecker for his memories and providing race facts; Werner Aichinger of Formula Koenig for his memories and for providing a wealth of material including photographs; Wolfgang Neumayer who handles German Formula 3 statistics; Manfred Hahn of German Formula 3; Daniel S Partel of EFDA; Graham Jones of Ford Motorsport Britain, and Helga Muller of Ford Germany; Dietmar Lenz of German karting; Maurice Hamilton of *The Observer*; Derick Allsop of *The Independent*; Malcolm Folley of *The Mail on Sunday*; Tony Jardine and Victoria Flack of Jardine PR; Mark Burgess for permission to quote from *Karting* magazine; Simon Taylor, the Managing Director of *Autosport* for permission to quote from that; Stephanie Chassagne of TAG-Heuer, the company whose statistical service is invaluable; Inga and Barbel for translation.

All pictures are courtesy of LAT, London, except where stated.

• CHAPTER ONE •

Weighty Matters

FROM LATE MARCH to late April 1995 Michael Schumacher's career resembled a looking-glass of chaos, confusion and controversy. At instants it deepened beyond even that and became a bitter, riven, volcanic thing. Could the crisp young man with the quasi-military haircut really be defending motor racing champion of the world?

There had been controversy before, of course, not least in the way Schumacher secured the Championship when he and Damon Hill crashed during the Australian Grand Prix of 13 November 1994, but by late April that afternoon at Adelaide six months before seemed remote, an episode from memory. Too much had happened in between.

It is true: 1995 ought to have been the settled season, governed by new rules to bring the purity of racing back to racing, and once the traditional (and faintly tedious) driver-team arrangements had been struck, the season did look primed with much more than the usual promise. Schumacher was joined at Benetton by the precocious Johnny Herbert, who'd done Japan and Australia for the team in '94 and had a full contract. Rothmans Williams kept Hill and gave David Coulthard a full contract rather than Nigel Mansell, who went to Marlboro McLaren partnering Mika Hakkinen. Ferrari made no changes, keeping Gerhard Berger and Jean Alesi, a strong duet for a team visibly strengthening. However, the kernel of the 16 races, beginning on 26 March, appeared to be Schumacher v Hill Part II, not least since Benetton now had the mighty Renault engines, as Williams did — but who knew? That was the promise.

Pre-seasons are ritualistic and formalised, new cars theatrically unveiled and tested hard, everyone cautious but openly optimistic. Benetton unveiled theirs in February, and Schumacher insisted that he wasn't feeling undue pressure despite so many people telling him he was clear favourite to retain the Championship. This is the sort of thing drivers insist, anyway. Schumacher did concede he'd moved from being 'the hunter to the hunted'. Benetton tested at Paul Ricard in the south of France where Schumacher did a best time of 1 minute 9.01 seconds, but Berger ran him close, no more than nine-hundredths slower. Williams were testing at Estoril and when Benetton went there it stayed close.

Schumacher	1:21.30
Irvine (Jordan)	1:21.67
Hill	1:21.75
Coulthard	1:21.75

The identical times of Hill and Coulthard are not, incidentally, a misprint, but one of those statistical astonishments that occasionally come along. Flavio Briatore, who runs Benetton, paid a flying visit, and during it Schumacher hacked out his hot lap. The team denied any 'conspiracy', insisting that it was just one of those coincidental astonishments that come along. Overall, and so far, nothing unusual.

With only a few days to the opener at Interlagos in Brazil, events at McLaren drowned contemplation of Schumacher v Hill Part II. To general astonishment, McLaren admitted that million-dollar Mansell wouldn't fit in the cockpit of their million-dollar car and wouldn't go to Brazil or the following race, Argentina. Schumacher, meanwhile, spoke in measured tones of how sensitive it would be returning to Brazil, the first race there since the death of Ayrton Senna at Imola in 1994. In sum, he anticipated a lively struggle with Hill. 'I feel more relaxed because I am champion.' Again this is the sort of thing drivers insist, anyway. Nothing unusual.

On the Thursday at Interlagos the drivers were weighed. In previous years the car had to be a minimum 515 kg, but under one of those

A man under pressure in 1995, almost daily pressure.

rule-changes the car and driver must now be a minimum 595 kg. This seemed straightforward and would work like this: the cars would be weighed again during the season but the drivers' weights from this Thursday would be taken as a constant — because they wouldn't vary much — and added. No point in weighing the drivers the whole time. Schumacher was 77 kg, which seemed mildly curious because at the beginning of 1994 he'd been 69. (A kilogram is 2.2 lbs, so he'd put on over a stone). Whatever, a man could clearly gain that over 12 months, as many of us know to our cost.

In Friday first qualifying Schumacher was sixth and pushing hard. In a corner he felt a 'little movement' from the car and in the next corner he had no steering at all. He missed the apex and the Benetton flowed onto grass. He reacted instinctively — so instinctively that subsequently he wasn't quite sure what he'd done — and changed down, making the car slew to strike a tyre wall backwards. The tyre wall shattered and scattered. Schumacher, shaken, said he wouldn't race unless the cause of the problem could be discovered and cured. It was, but only after much consternation at anticipating Schumacher v Hill minus Schumacher.

In second qualifying Schumacher went quickest, but not quick enough to dislodge Hill who'd taken provisional pole on the Friday. Schumacher led the race until he pitted on lap 18, ceding the lead to Hill, but on lap 30 Hill's gearbox seized and he spun off. Schumacher pitted a second time, ceding the lead to Coulthard, but regained it when Coulthard pitted and never lost it. He beat Coulthard by some 8 seconds. Nothing unusual, another Schumacher win. He'd set off any minute for a relaxing break on the coast.

'For a team to say one of their competitors is cheating I find shocking'

Before that, he was weighed again (a spot check) and the scales said 71.5 kg. This would cause an eruption, although not before a different eruption. Five hours after the race — Schumacher long departed, and Coulthard too — the FIA, the sport's governing body, announced that Elf fuel samples taken from the Benetton and Williams did not match the fuel samples previously submitted for approval. Schumacher and Coulthard were stripped of their points pending appeals by the teams. While Formula 1 tried to ingest this, word emerged of what the scales said and a ringing question was born that anyone who has ever dieted found fascinating. How could Schumacher be 77 kg on Thursday and 71.5 on Sunday? It was tempting to be flippant about this (has he sold the secret to Weight Watchers?) but the temptation had to be resisted. It was too serious in its implication. Without the Sunday check, 77 would have been added to the car during the season rather than 71.5. Patrick Head, the Williams designer, estimated that pulling 5.5 kg less meant around 14 seconds gained over a race.

Many mischievous theories were put forward, but Heiner Bickinger, Schumacher's PR, countered. 'First of all he had a couple of days off before Brazil. He went to the Club Med and they have a pretty good French cuisine. He likes to eat, and he likes to eat good. Therefore when he arrived at the racetrack he had one or two more kilos than usual. Secondly he didn't have his race helmet when he was on the scales, because that didn't arrive until Friday — but that's only a few hundred grammes. He drank between two and three litres of water, and you can translate one litre of water to one kilo of weight, as part of his fitness programme. That was coupled with some salt tablets to keep the water in the body and make the blood thin. He's naturally losing between one and two kilos during the race, and if you watched I think you saw that the car wasn't good at all compared to the Williams and Ferrari. He had to work a lot harder than the other drivers.' Schumacher said, 'I certainly did not go to the toilet before the weigh-in.' Surely billion-dollar Grand Prix racing hadn't come to this?

Following Brazil, Gerhard Berger (third, a lap down, but promoted to first pending the appeals) caused an aftershock when he seemed to say in a British newspaper that 'cheating is cheating'. Berger pointed out that what he actually said was 'rules are rules', something self-evidently true and not the same thing. The 'cheating is cheating', however, stung Michel Bonnet, Elf's head of marketing, to a trenchant response. 'For a team to say that one of their competitors is cheating, and for the drivers to say that, I find shocking.'

Schumacher holidayed at Bahia, Brazil. During it he went out in a boat to dive a coral reef. Fiancé Corinna Betsch and manager Willi Weber remained on the boat while Schumacher made the dive — with an instructor, a hotel manager and his trainer Harry Hawkela — 8 miles off the coast. The boat drifted and when Schumacher came up it had moved out of sight.

'It was a terrible feeling. The waves were quite big. In the beginning I was screaming to get together and take hands trying to get to the boat, but we didn't move and it was difficult with the waves taking us backwards and forwards. I felt I could go quicker by myself. I opened up the belt with the weights and threw that away and I was thinking of taking off the air bottle but I didn't know how to do that without losing the life vest, which was with it, so in the end I tried to swim with the bottle. The other three guys were almost finished. They were just lying on the water with their life vests on. Corinna saw me first.'

Schumacher had swum for an hour to make sure he and the others were picked up safely.

'For the first time in my life, I thought that was it,' Schumacher said. 'For the first time I got scared, really scared. When I had the accident in Brazil, for example, where I suddenly had no steering, it didn't scare me. It happened, we had an explanation for it, we resolved it. I feel comfortable in a racing car, where I know what I'm doing, but I've never thought about death before.'

No Grand Prix had been held in Argentina since 1981, for a variety of financial and political reasons. Coulthard took pole, Hill alongside, Schumacher on the second row. Coulthard led but had problems, drifted back, seemed to overcome the problems and drew up to Schumacher, outbraked him and overtook him. In the course of this move Schumacher seemed to back off. For a driver so strong and uncompromising, this might be revealing. Hill drove a magnificent race to win from Alesi, Schumacher third. Schumacher made three pit stops and explained that 'there was a lot of variation in the performance depending on the tyres. On the first and third set of tyres I was nowhere, but on the last set everything was perfect and I was able to set fastest lap of the race. If I had had four sets like that I think I could have won.'

By now the German Press had rounded on Schumacher, and the German Press, like the German Police, are not be to trifled with. He arrived in Buenos Aires and complained that 'no one talked about what a great race I had in Brazil. They wrote of other things. I am getting to the point where I find these accusations too much to take. There are limits. I have thought about going to IndyCars. I was thinking about it before Brazil, but certainly thinking about it afterwards.' Sabre-rattling? Pique? A serious intent to go to the USA? The pressure of the eruptions? Certainly the formalistic, quietened days of the unveiling of the new car and testing it seemed as far away as Adelaide.

On the Thursday after Argentina, the FIA Appeals Committee met in Paris and re-instated the Schumacher and Coulthard points. Elf expressed satisfaction.

'After detailed examination of the technical problem which took place at the Brazilian Grand Prix and which brought about the

Right *An early lead in Argentina, the Williams predatory.* (ICN UK Bureau)

disqualification of Michael Schumacher, Benetton Renault, and David Coulthard, Williams Renault, both teams and their petroleum partner Elf confirm, in the light of the information they have obtained so far, that the difference in the original fuel sample sent to the FIA for approval and the fuel used by the two teams at the Brazilian Grand Prix was due to a difference in the sampling procedures.

'They acknowledge that the chromatographic [dividing components of a mixture] procedures used by the FIA and the equipment which was used was correct and that some statements made to the press by Elf and the teams were based on information that was received prior to knowledge of the results of the new analysis.

'The FIA have confirmed that the fuel used by the two teams was completely legal and they acknowledge that no advantage was obtained by the fuel used by the teams and that there was no intention to infringe the regulation. The decision of the stewards was based on the fact that the chromatogram of the fuel used at the event was not identical to the chromatogram of the sample that was sent by Elf for approval by the FIA.'

Another eruption, despite fines of $200,000 on Benetton and Williams. Niki Lauda, the former World Champion and currently Ferrari adviser, said, 'I cannot separate car and driver completely. If this is the new rule, you can build an illegal car and let the team pay for victory. The whole thing is only commercial and has nothing to do with sport any more. It's like scoring a half-goal in soccer — it is not possible. Either you score a goal or not. The decision for me is the biggest defeat for the FIA, who cannot govern the sport any longer.' Berger put it more bluntly, as well he might. 'I no longer understand anything. Formula 1 has become a joke.'

Table after Argentina		*Table after Paris*	
Berger	11	Schumacher	14
Hill	10	Hill	10
Alesi	10	Alesi	8
Hakkinen	6	Coulthard	6
Schumacher	4	Berger	5

Before Imola Schumacher was quoted as saying that 'Berger should concentrate on racing instead of thinking how he can criticise me. If

Berger drove with the talent he shows doing his own PR, he would have won many more races. I have never understood how somebody could celebrate a victory like that [Brazil] one lap down and winning after someone else has been disqualified.'

Berger struck back a day later. 'I never criticised Schumacher. I only criticised the decision [to reinstate him]. I can live with Schumacher being angry. I was declared the winner by the FIA stewards so I had every reason to open the champagne.' Berger also referred to the podium after the San Marino Grand Prix of 1994: the race had been restarted after Senna's accident and Schumacher won. 'I cannot understand how someone can celebrate a victory by jumping around when one of our colleagues has died.' Berger described this jumping around as 'like a clown' and also said he objected to champagne being sprayed. Schumacher struck back at that. 'Berger has a short memory. First, there was no champagne. Second, Senna's death was only announced later.' Before Imola, Schumacher and Berger met in a gym in Monte Carlo and smoothed out their differences.

'Leading the race, then throwing it at the wall is not the sort of thing Michael does'

At Imola FIA President Max Mosley gave a Press Conference and admonished Schumacher. 'I think it is unfortunate that the World Champion gets involved in a misunderstanding about how much he may or may not weigh at any time on a race weekend. It reflects poorly on the sport and shows lack of an adult attitude. It's not extraordinary that somebody should put on a stone over a year, particularly as weight no longer matters and they've been doing a lot of training and so on. What is extraordinary is that he should lose it in three days. It was a pity that it became a matter for public discussion, whether he drank a huge amount of water, didn't go to the loo or had a heavy helmet. It is just a pity he didn't take care that it didn't happen.' Schumacher struck back at *that*. During the weekend he met Mosley. 'I told him that in future it might be good if he had a word with me before [he said such things], so he can judge from the facts.'

Schumacher took pole, although under the weight of Senna's memory confessed that he'd rather the race had been somewhere else.

Pole was decided on the Friday — hotter weather on the Saturday precluded improvements — in a hectic, thrusting session. Alesi, Hill and Coulthard all went quickest at one stage or another, but Schumacher capped them with 1:27.478, which he immediately lowered to 1:27.274. Berger made a (literal) last-second rush at this and squeezed 1:27.282, a difference of 0.008 over the 3-mile circuit. A Schumacher-Berger front row seemed potentially alarming in view of what they'd been saying about each other and because the corner where Senna crashed — the first after the green light — had been refashioned and tightened to allow only one car through at a time . . .

It rained on race morning and the front runners chose wet tyres. Schumacher made a mighty, monumental start, Berger tucked in behind. They threaded safely through, the cars nervy as the tyres sought grip. Schumacher felt confident that he could 'control' Berger. Soon enough a dry line appeared and Berger pitted for slicks on lap 5, leaving Schumacher 2.104 seconds ahead of Coulthard. Schumacher pitted for slicks on lap 10 and emerged third behind Coulthard and Berger. Moving towards Piratella, the hard left on the far side of the circuit, Schumacher lost the Benetton. It spun on the grass, struck a wall, spun on, bounded across a run-off area partially in the air and thrashed a tyre barrier. Schumacher clambered out quickly and trotted from the scene. 'After the tyre change I felt that the car was a bit unstable at the rear. It's not clear why I went off and we will have to investigate the reason. I was afraid because it's a really quick part of the circuit and it felt as if the spinning was never going to stop.' Hill won to have a total of 20 points, Schumacher still on 14.

One aspect seemed clear. The Benetton's chassis was not yet as good as the Williams, suggesting that Schumacher was having to dig too deep into himself to compensate. Another aspect did not seem clear. Were the accumulating pressure of this *and* the almost daily controversies exacting a toll? Schumacher's race engineer Pat Symonds said lustily, 'Michael knows damn well that if you get into a race and your car is not capable of winning but is capable of finishing second, then you get six points and that's what counts at the end of the year. Maybe Michael did make a mistake — people do — but if he did I don't think it was necessarily the result of pressure. Leading the race then throwing it at the wall is not the sort of thing Michael does.'

In Spain Schumacher gave his own answer, but not before Hill had said of him, 'I know he has a certain amount of arrogance, but I don't believe he is impervious to criticism. At the weigh-in in Brazil he was pushing the regulations, and effectively stuck two fingers up at them. That is not the sort of behaviour you expect from a champion. He has been making mistakes, too, which is the sign of someone over-driving.' Schumacher's answer? He dug deep to take pole on the Saturday (1:21.452 against Alesi's 1:22.052, Hill fifth on 1:22.349) and — discounting the diversion of pit stops — led the race from beginning to end making no semblance of a mistake. Hill, a distant second until the final lap when he lost hydraulic pressure, came fourth. That gave Schumacher the Championship lead, 24–23.

At Monaco Hill took a tight pole from Schumacher, 0.790 of a second between them but potentially decisive if Hill reached the first corner in the lead; he did. Schumacher pressured for a while then fell back for what seemed a pleasant Sunday afternoon run and six points. Hill pitted for new tyres and fuel — the first of two stops — and Schumacher would follow any lap now. Wouldn't he? Schumacher

Could he take the pressure? Yes, he stormed Spain. (ICN UK Bureau)

went hard to build a gap before his stop and this became wondrous to behold, the shark-nosed Benetton oscillating under power, quivering towards the metal barriers, bounding over the bumps as it searched out its prey; and that prey was time itself, the car swallowing the seconds that ought to have belonged to Hill. And lap on lap on lap Schumacher did not come in.

Only then was it clear, the masterstroke. Schumacher intended to stop only once and, if he could sustain his pace until then, Hill faced a crippling disadvantage from which he could not recover — the time lost in his extra pit stop. Schumacher flew onwards and won it by 35 seconds. Yes, he'd say, a pleasant Sunday afternoon run, and pleasanter in the Championship: 34–29, Hill visibly downcast.

Hill would be more than downcast in Canada. Schumacher had pole and led comfortably from Hill, who fell back into the clutches of the Ferraris and was overtaken by them before the hydraulic pump failed after 50 laps. As he emerged from the cockpit his whole body was consumed by rage. He'd been third at the time, four points gone. Nor was he mollified when on lap 57 Schumacher crawled into the pits stuck in third gear; a new steering wheel (they contain the gear shift mechanism) was fitted and Schumacher burned a path from seventh to fifth — and two points. Schumacher 36–29 and the pressure all tilted on to Hill.

Schumacher had been almost mechanical in his mastery at Montreal until circumstances beyond his control intervened. That was one aspect of him. Monaco distilled another aspect, distilled — in fact — the core of this book. Not just the arguments and fines and suspensions but the utterly gifted racing driver making his statement. *Here are my gifts, savour them . . .*

• CHAPTER TWO •

Kick Start

THE BEGINNING HOLDS a lovely glimpse of innocence. Picture it. A kart propelled by a lawnmower engine puttering down an ordinary street and hitting a lamp-post. Lots of kids crash their karts. A certain Nigel Mansell did, for instance, on a garage forecourt while his father negotiated to buy it. He hit a petrol pump.

Michael Schumacher's journey to the lamp-post started when he was given a pedal-powered kart at the age of four, but after his parents added the engine and he crashed, they thought he'd be safer on a proper track. Schumacher was born to Rolf and Elisabeth on 3 January 1969 at Hurth-Hermulheim near Cologne and brought up in Kerpen, a town of 54,000 inhabitants slightly further away from Cologne. Rolf was a housebuilder, Schumacher says, 'not a rich man. We went into motor racing in the cheapest possible way, go-karting'. Kerpen had a track.

The chance to drive regularly feeds on itself. The more mastery a youngster acquires the more the satisfaction and desire to extend that mastery. Karting, an exciting pastime, may lead nowhere in particular. Later there'll be a job to find and protect, and the only evidence will lie in a drawer somewhere — curling amateurish photographs of the boy buzzing round some track on a hornet of a thing. In time, however, Schumacher's parents would manage the track at Kerpen . . .

Many years hence, Schumacher partnered Riccardo Patrese at Benetton in Formula 1 and this partnership acted as a bridge of the generations. Patrese made his Grand Prix debut in 1977 when Schumacher was eight. Schumacher says that at that age 'I never even knew about Grand Prix racing, only about karting. I didn't set out to become a German sports star like Boris Becker or Steffi Graf but more just to enjoy myself. My hero was Toni Schumacher (no relation), the goalkeeper who played for Cologne and the national team. I always wanted to be like him. I took my football very seriously, especially between the ages of 12 and 15 when I copied him and played in goal all the time'.

The beauty about karting is that it is comparatively cheap and if you're good you move up in a natural progression without risk of bankruptcy. Of all forms of motorsport, it is arguably the most democratic because merit is more important than money. The moving up — to national championships and international competitions — involves a sequence of conjunctions with strangers whose careers will interweave across the future. In 1980 Schumacher and family went to Nivelles in Belgium to watch the World Kart Championships. A certain Ayrton Senna finished second . . .

'When I was 10 or 12, I couldn't do serious racing because I was too young. Over the weekends, when other people were at the track and it was raining and nobody wanted to drive, I always said *come on, let me drive, let me drive*. I enjoyed those conditions, playing with the kart, making 360 degree turns. That's the best way for getting the feeling for a kart or a car. Racing in the rain is difficult, that's true, but you just have to be careful and handle the situation.

'I had the childhood of any other boy, playing football, climbing trees, getting into a little trouble. Absolutely normal. Then one weekend when I was around 11 I had to decide whether to take part in a judo competition or a go-kart race. I chose judo, came third and I knew I had made the wrong decision. Even then, racing was a hobby. I had no fantasies about Grands Prix.'

Most Formula 1 drivers start in karts. Reflecting on this,

Right *This sporting life. As a youngster Schumacher followed his namesake Toni Schumacher, West Germany's goalkeeper. As a Formula 1 driver, Michael played for the drivers' team.*

Schumacher says 'people keep asking me how it is I can come into Formula 1 and establish myself so quickly near the top level and for me there is a simple answer: experience. Although I am very young compared to some of the other drivers, I have spent a long time in motorsport, 19 years altogether, and I have had really good preparation for the job. After all, I did 15 years in karts from 1973 to 1988 and in that time I drove a lot of races, got myself into so many situations and learned so many things, like driving wheel-to-wheel, close to other people and fighting and so on. I got used to it. (Fighting means a hard but hopefully fair contest between drivers.) We had tyre situations, too, with soft compounds which I had to learn about as well, how to take it easy and not push them too hard in the beginning or they would be finished at the end; and also a lot about tactics. All the lessons were well learned and I used them in my further career. I enjoyed karts because you drive bumper-to-bumper and this is real racing'.

'Although I am very young I have spent a long time in motorsport'

The youngster is absorbing a reservoir of craft which has direct application later on if he is one of the very rare ones who goes on to make a career in motorsport.

'I first met Michael in karting at Kerpen when I was 15 and he was 12,' Heinz-Harald Frentzen says, and here is the interweaving. Many years hence, Frentzen would become a rival in Formula 1. When he split up with his girlfriend Corinna Betsch she moved in with Schumacher. 'I did the German Junior Championships in 1981 and the next year I raced against Michael at Kerpen,' says Frentzen. 'He only did that one race and was what you might call a "guest starter". I didn't race against him again until Formula 3.'

'It is not right to say we grew up together,' says Otto Rensing, who'd also become a Formula 3 rival, 'although in one sense we did. I started karting in 1977 and I knew about Michael, I knew about the circuit at Kerpen that his parents ran. I live about 25 kilometres from there. I started at another circuit and won club races. The new circuit at Kerpen opened in 1978 or 1979 and I changed clubs and went there.

That's when I got to know Michael. What was he like then? A "little giant" of the man who ran the circuit, his father. I was 17, he seven years younger. At one point I think I can say I was very successful in karting, the most successful in Germany, and I did that up to 24 when I started motor racing, so the last years of that I saw Michael growing up.'

The interweaving can also mean separating. In 1994, while Schumacher won Grand Prix after Grand Prix, Rensing reflected on how he could get himself into Formula 1; and so did a lively Scotsman, Allan McNish.

'I went to the 1983 World Junior Championships as a spectator, at Kerpen, the circuit his father ran,' McNish says. 'That was the first time I'd seen Michael race. He raced the year after — 1984 — but I was ill and couldn't compete. (Schumacher won the German Junior title that year, his initial championship victory.) The first time we came up against each other was at the Junior World Championships at Le Mans in 1985, the little kart circuit right opposite Maison Blanche and the Porsche Curve' (two famous landmarks on the full circuit).

The story of Michael Schumacher is in a very real sense a mystery story, not a *whodunnit* but a *howdunnit?*

I understand, I hope, how Mansell forged himself into a great driver (blood, sweat and tears), how Prost thought himself into a great driver (reason and logic), how Senna levitated himself into a great driver (God and God-given gifts burned into an obsession). Mansell slogged through endless setbacks, Prost overcame setbacks, Senna we had watched — through FF1600, F2000, F3 and an F1 year of promise with Toleman — gather into a hurricane, but entirely visible long before it arrived.

Schumacher, it seemed, simply arrived. He was there all at once, bright and chirpy, fair and lean, clean cut, bearing with him the delight he could not or did not camouflage in victory. Just as suddenly, people murmured about his ability in direct comparison to that of Senna. He did come from somewhere, of course, and that was initially karting, and then the lesser formulae single-seater racing. Examining those early races leads to an understanding of the child, born to an ordinary, everyday household who matured to immense fortune and far-reaching fame but remained recognisably what he had always been: straightforward, honest, *normal.*

He claimed no great talent for the game, but he looks composed on the ball, doesn't he?

The World Juniors at Le Mans in 1985 ran to a complicated format, which for simplicity can be described as two self-contained days of racing. On the first, *Karting* magazine reported that 'the driver who dominated the heats was Allan McNish with three excellent wins and a second place from row four. Section A: Although McNish was on pole, Schumacher shot straight into the lead never to be headed. Allan threatened occasionally but never looked likely to get past.

'Pre-Final. The group winners, (Yvan) Muller, Schumacher and (Gianluca) Beggio lined up at the front with Muller on pole. McNish was on the second row. The first corner saw a six-kart pile-up, due in the main to the very fast starts that were allowed. Muller led with Beggio, Schumacher, McNish and the rest chasing'. Muller won from Schumacher.

'Final: Schumacher was away, followed by Muller, Beggio, (Andrea) Gilardi, McNish and (Massimiliano) Orsini and for the next five laps or so the leaders chopped and changed.' Gilardi won from Schumacher.

In the last of the qualifying races on day two, 'Gilardi, trying to make it seven victories out of seven starts, led them away. Gilardi briefly lost his lead to Schumacher, but successfully recaptured it. Later Schumacher was off at the end of the main straight but managed to restart in tenth. He started to fight his way back when he was given the mechanical malfunction flag and made to retire'.

Leading qualifiers, in order: Muller, Gilardi, McNish, Schumacher. A certain Christian Fittipaldi, who'd journeyed from Brazil for the Championships, didn't make it, didn't interweave yet.

In the Pre-Final 'Gilardi made yet another of his good starts with Muller, Schumacher and McNish following, and then pulled out a substantial lead. Schumacher overtook Muller and the latter retired soon afterwards. By lap 7 McNish was all over Schumacher and then got past but was unable to shake off the very determined German who kept up the pressure'.

McNish says 'my inexperience took over, or the experience of the rest took over. I didn't make a very good start, I wasn't quite up to speed. Schumacher passed me and got into second place and from then on it was Gilardi, Schumacher and myself to the flag. I was with him but I couldn't do anything about it. All the way through the meeting we had been closely matched'.

Karting reported that 'at the start Schumacher tagged onto Gilardi and squeezed in front of McNish. Schumacher was desperately trying to get in an overtaking position but Gilardi looked in absolute control of the race. By their sheer pace they had opened up a small gap over McNish. In the closing stages Schumacher gave all he had but still Gilardi held him off and took the flag, a worthy retainer of the title. Schumacher looked bitterly disappointed but on the day didn't have quite enough to stop the flying Italian. McNish had impressed everybody'.

What sort of a chap was Schumacher then? 'Quite different to now,' McNish says. 'We were both 15 or 16, pretty young. He drove very much on natural talent and whereas he still has the same flair he uses his mind a lot more and he is strong technically as well. He drives like an extremely mature man. In karting he hadn't developed that aspect. He was a quick, hard racer — as everybody was at that stage — and he was the one you knew would be there or thereabouts in the races. I competed against him again in 1985 in the Italian Grand Prix, as it was called, at Parma, one of the most famous kart tracks in Italy. Schumacher was second again and I was third again!

'I can only really remember speaking to him at the Junior Worlds very briefly after one of the pre-finals or one of the races I'd just won. I had a little chat. He spoke very much broken English but to be honest, none of the drivers really socialised. One reason was that we were so young and our native languages were the only ones we spoke with any confidence. It's only later, when an overseas driver's career begins to rise, that he learns English.

'The other reason is that we were competing against each other and battling hard against each other. For major meetings, we didn't tend to be social about it — we took it extremely seriously. It was probably as serious then as Formula 3 is now. It's quite funny, because I only did the European and World Championship events (outside the UK), so every time I went it was different people to beat, although Gilardi was usually the one. A couple of years ago I looked back through a Formula 3000 grid and it was extremely strange. Basically, all the people I'd raced in karts were on that grid, people like Gianni Morbidelli and so on.'

Elmar Hoffmann, a German official, remembers that 'Schumacher was never a brilliant kart driver — very good but not as a young man

This sporting life. The cyclist, leading — and winning — a charity race at Silverstone.

so good that you'd say he would become a Formula 1 driver. But what we know is that drivers who are not so good in karting can be very, very good in car racing. He worked hard and he was a funny boy, he made jokes with his friends, but he was never one who worked against the rules, not a type who is tricky or who tries to cheat. He was always correct, fair and correct. And always polite'.

Only one driver who reached Formula 1 won the World Karting Championship as well — Patrese.

As Rensing watched Schumacher grow, 'for long years I had the lap records at Kerpen, all the lap records, and then suddenly that changed. Michael Schumacher beat them. People said he was good and I could see he was good because he broke my lap records. I met him and spoke to him but because of the difference in ages there was not so much we had in common'.

In 1986 Schumacher came third in the German Senior Championships, spread over six rounds, although he only finished in four. A certain Karl Wendlinger, from Kufstein in Austria, came fifteenth.

'That season,' McNish says, 'the European Championships were over two rounds, the first in Sweden and the second in Germany. In Sweden — Gothenburg — I hate to say it but Schumacher finished second and I finished third again! We both went onto Dunlop tyres, which weren't the ones for the circuit. A Danish driver caller Gert Munkholm won on Bridgestones. Schumacher and I both struggled with understeer.'

Karting, reporting the final, said that 'McNish in second place was obviously struggling to hold off Schumacher and eventually succumbed to a nice out-braking move on the hairpin. Schumacher pulled out a few lengths but couldn't quite get away. The rest of the field were well back so Frank Van Eglem (a Dutchman) could concentrate on the job in hand and towards the end of the race passed both Schumacher and McNish. But spurred on by Terry Fullerton (an experienced karter and McNish's mentor) leaning over the fence and making threatening gestures, the young Scot got back into contact and when Van Eglem was demoralised by Schumacher doing the out-braking trick at the hairpin, pulled the same move on him the next time round'.

At Oppenrod, which someone described as a 'very convoluted track' near Frankfurt, Schumacher won the heats from Alessandro Zanardi and Emanuelle Naspetti, McNish 42nd. 'Allan had a dreadful set of heats for various reasons,' *Karting* said, preferring not to elaborate.

'To be honest,' McNish says, 'I can't remember who came where in the final because my brake disc broke and I didn't finish so it wasn't a real interest to me. I do remember Schumacher didn't win because a Swede did.'

That was Linus Lundberg. *Karting* reported that 'Schumacher made the most of his pole position and went streaking away. Lundberg grabbed second. Once free of the others, Lundberg reeled in Schumacher and put him under tremendous pressure. Lundberg's relentless pressure brought forth fruit as he squirmed past Schumacher to then open up an enormous lead which he never looked like losing.

(Ralf) Kelleners challenged Schumacher. For six laps they fought until Kelleners got through. Schumacher was again put under pressure, this time from Munkholm, but managed to hold on to take third'.

In 1987 Schumacher came second in the European Championship northern zone heat, this time at a circuit called Genk 'which is actually situated at a little sleepy town called Horensbergdam'. *Karting* reported that 'the pits could have been better, with most teams situated in a field some distance from the dummy grid and having a long treck on a muddy path'. In the opening time trials section 'the surprise package of the day was the pretty young girl driver, Lotta Hellberg from Sweden, whose second timed lap was all that prevented her from gaining pole position for all her races'.

'Schumacher gave us an indication of what he intended to do when he disappeared into the distance early on'

Fifteen heats followed. In the third 'Schumacher gave us an indication of what he intended to do this weekend when he disappeared into the distance early on'. In the final 'after one false start it was (Rene) Bollingtoft who took the lead from Conny Eriksson, Schumacher and (Robert) Valkenburg. On lap 3, Schumacher passed Eriksson on the infield loop and set about catching Bollingtoft whose advantage was slowly disappearing. On lap 10 Schumacher made a daring move on the back straight and took the lead. Next time round Bollingtoft tried the same, but to no effect as Schumacher firmly shut the door in his face.

'The gap between the two packs at the front had again narrowed and when Bollingtoft tried to pass Schumacher at turn one, (Martijn) Koene slipped up the inside of both of them and pulled away slightly. Schumacher was to have none of this and pulled away from Bollingtoft. Koene and Schumacher now had command at the front and try as he might Schumacher could not pass Koene who drove some of the best blocking lines I have seen for some time to take the flag after 24 gruelling laps'.

The European Championship Final, drawing the Northern and Southern Zones together, was at Gothenburg with an entry of more than 100. Schumacher led after the heats and in the pre-final took a

The tennis player: strength and timing.

comfortable lead. In the final 'from his pole position Schumacher again took the lead, followed by Frederico Gemmo and Bollingtoft. On lap three Orsini and Zanardi were in the lead and started a fight that will go down in karting history. Several times they overtook each other and several times they went through bends side by side. At the beginning of lap 22 of a 24 lap race Zanardi was in the lead.

'Orsini was faster on the long straight so Zanardi tried to keep him behind by driving to the right on the straight. But this did not stop Orsini. He attacked where there was not enough room for both of them and the two Italians took each other off the track. Zanardi wanted to finish the race and pushed his kart to restart it. Orsini's father ran out and tried to stop him by kicking him in the back. With the two Italians out of the race, the victory and the European Championship title was handed to Michael Schumacher who tactically concentrated on keeping Bollingtoft and Gemmo behind him'.

Kicks in the back? Zanardi remembers them. 'We did all the race, Orsini and I, passing each other and on the last lap, well, he did a small mistake in the corner before the straight and he knew that it was his final chance to take the lead. I saw him about 25, 30 metres behind me. I thought "that's it, I've won" because I knew he wouldn't be able to overtake me on the straight. Then he did a desperate manoeuvre. He didn't brake at all! He went directly into my kart and we both went off. I was trying to restart because I had a big advantage — 27 seconds — over Schumacher and if I'd been able to restart I could still have won. His father came along and started to kick me, that's absolutely right.'

Karting reported that 'after the race a calm Schumacher commented "I regret the outcome. I waited lap after lap for the two fighting Italians to do something stupid, and they did".' Directly after the final Bollingtoft protested Schumacher. 'After two warm-up laps the German driver had noticed that his engine was loose on the chassis. He had tightened it up before the start but the rules say that you are not allowed to get any help on the track. The Stewards rejected the protest due to the fact that Schumacher tightened the bolts himself and did not receive any outside help. Bollingtoft said afterwards that he was satisfied with the decision and added that he would not have wanted to be champion in this way'.

Zanardi made a protest against Orsini 'and then the Italian

Federation came to me because he was one of the top Italian drivers. They said "well, you know, if you go through with this protest it's going to be a big problem" so I retired the protest and then what happened? In the Italian Championships he ran me off and I lost that one, too . . .'

That season Schumacher locked into a struggle with a driver called Peter Hantscher in German Senior Karting. Schumacher won the opening round at Kerpen, Hantscher the second round at a place called Geesthacht. 'How? Easy. I was a bit faster than him! I'd known him before the season, although I began karting at Munich and he at Kerpen, but I'd seen him literally take his first faltering steps into the sport. That season was the biggest fight of my life and exceptional in that two Germans were struggling for our own Championship.' The Dane Munkholm had won it the season before. 'It was the best time of my racing career and maybe the best time for Schumacher, too, a very hard fight but a very, very fair one and, if you want the truth, tremendous fun measuring each other's strength. We always shook hands in friendship.'

'When it was over we were still friends and we still shook hands'

They approached the eighth and final round at a place called Walldorf with Hantscher needing to win and Schumacher needing a single point for the Championship. 'He set fastest time in qualifying and I set second fastest time,' Hantscher says. 'I was absolutely determined to win or have an accident. I would not give in, I really wouldn't give in. I repeat: I would have preferred a collision.'

Before the race Schumacher murmured to himself 'don't do anything wrong, make sure you finish'.

Hantscher remembers what happened next. 'It was tense, wheel-to-wheel, no, tyrewall-to-tyrewall, and then Schumacher fell back a little. To show you what we were drawing out of each other, the third driver finished 150 metres behind. When it was over we were still friends and we still shook hands.' Schumacher, second, had the Championship from Hantscher, 127 points to 112.

During the season a Lamborghini dealer in Germany called Gustav

Hoecker noticed Schumacher and thought 'this is a nice guy, he handles a kart perfectly'. Hoecker would not forget Schumacher when he — Hoecker — came to choose a driver for Formula Koenig, which is car racing. Meanwhile Peter Sieber, who'd been mechanic to Heinz-Harald Frentzen in karting and was now heavily involved in a Formula Ford team called EUFRA, noticed Schumacher too. Sieber 'said to Michael "maybe you'd like to try a single-seater one time" and he said "yes, I'd like that!"'

Hoffmann, in his capacity as a karting official, regrets that you can race single-seaters at 16, two years before the legal age limit on the roads. It tends to lure karters away from karting when, if they stayed, the two further years would give them a chance to capitalize on their experience and maybe win international championships. In sum, he says, 'youngsters start in single-seaters very early if their parents have the money'. Schumacher's parents didn't, but it scarcely mattered if a Lamborghini importer or an enthusiast like Sieber wanted to give him a chance.

'Michael had already had contact with a couple of teams but that came to nothing because, I think, he had no money,' Sieber says. 'Towards the end of 1987 — I remember it was a cold day — Michael came to Hockenheim to drive our Formula Ford 1600 car, his first time in a single-seater. I said to one of the team owners "OK, you drive the car and then Michael drives it and if he is quicker than you, we have to do something for him". Michael was quicker. He told me what he felt in the car and I thought "oh, he feels a lot of things in the car, he doesn't just drive it".' Sieber thought again.

Schumacher remembers 'the year after I won the German and European championships I got an offer to drive for money — which is rare in karts. Then, suddenly, I also got the offer of a Formula Ford test and it went from there. I was warned that karters sometimes don't adapt well to FF1600, but I was on the pace straight away. I did 25 laps and the only comparison I had was with the EUFRA owner, who used to be quite quick and raced with Keke Rosberg. After I'd done a time, he said that it must be a very good day for driving, got in the car and was 2.5 seconds slower. We got down to some negotiations and that was it'.

A footnote from McNish, capturing the interweaving. 'I spoke to

Michael last year (1993) and it was funny recounting some of the things that happened in the past, just talking about people we'd both known and who we were involved with during that period. We were looking back from our different points of view — and looking through our own little rose-tinted spectacles at the age of 23, 24 — into the good old days of karting. It's also funny how you remember some drivers and not others. I did remember Michael and I do remember Paul Tracy (now a leading IndyCar driver). Paul and his father came over from Canada and Paul competed in a race I was in in Lincolnshire.

'I went into Formula Ford 1600 in 1987 but Michael stayed in karts. In November, December time I went over to a circuit in France to demonstrate the Van Diemen to various teams there (who were potential customers for Van Diemens) so that they'd see the 1987 car was quicker than the 1986. The '87 car came straight from Hockenheim and the driver who drove it there was Schumacher, his first run in a single-seater . . .'

A footnote. In 1994 Schumacher visited the little community of Manheim near Kerpen (not to be confused with Mannheim, the big city a long way south) because a group of supporters wanted to salute his achievements. They agreed that he didn't really come from Manheim but they were adopting him anyway. An old woman took him to one side and said 'there is a candle burning for you in the chapel whenever you are racing'. Schumacher, meanwhile, said to the assembly that he hoped they'd forgive him for all the noise from the kart track. Strictly speaking, it's closer to Manheim than Kerpen.

A footnote from Rensing. 'At karting meetings I didn't know all the other 30 drivers, only the ones who were good. That is normal in karting and normal in some other forms of racing, too. Later on I met people in Formula 3000 and all the young guys like Zanardi knew me but I didn't know them — because I was quite a central figure in karting, I was the one they looked out for. I didn't remember them because they were growing up.'

A footnote from Hantscher. 'Schumacher was a very upright young man, friendly, ready to help. I'm still active in German karting. I stopped competing for five years to build up a business dealing in karts but I'm competing again now (1994) in the German Championship. If we meet we greet each other just like we did in the old times despite the fact that he's in Formula 1. Schumacher's hobby became Formula 1 and Hantscher's hobby became his business!'

A footnote from Zanardi. 'Schumacher was a very good kart driver, although obviously not as good as he is now in Formula 1. For me, he used to be a good challenger but quite honestly I have to say that in karting I had very good material and that's why I was quicker than him all the time. Also most of the material was made in Italy so we got the chance to do a lot of testing, maybe two or three times a week, which helped. The atmosphere between the drivers was like a big, big family. The drivers knew each other and especially before the races we socialised very, very well. We stayed together even the evening before a race, we played billiards and things like that. Basically we lived at the circuits and you didn't have all of this pressure you get from the Press and so on in Formula 1. Many times you'd sleep in the

They competed from the early days. Schumacher and Karl Wendlinger.

motorhome or in a van.' (Compare with McNish and 'none of the drivers really socialised'. It depends on who you were, how you were and what you remember.)

The Schumachers produced a single page publicity sheet in 1987 to advertise his potential. Michael Schumacher sits bare-headed on a kart, his face serious. The kart bears the number 1 and the caption says European Champion. It lists his karting record and directs anyone interested to contact Rolf Schumacher at their address in Kerpen. Potential sponsors, no doubt.

Courtesy of Gustav Hoecker's judgement, or perhaps intuition, the photographs of the buzzing hornets could go in the drawer. Schumacher would never drive a kart again except for purest pleasure, which he indulged himself in even when he'd reached Formula 1. The career was getting serious.

• CHAPTER THREE •

Sign
Here Please

HERE'S A LITTLE history recounted by Werner Aichinger, who now runs Formula Koenig, the conduit into single-seaters. 'There's a man called Richard Koenig who makes car and sports seats and also has a great big heart for pushing new drivers. He was in Italy in 1986 and saw Formula Panda running there. He said to himself "this is a formula we don't have in Germany". He asked who built the cars and was told it was a company in Milan. He went there and said "build me 40 cars but keep them in kit form so that the guys who buy them can learn about them as they put them together".

'He bought the 40 cars and sold them and in the middle of 1987 we had the first Formula Koenig cars, as they were called. They had Fiat engines and Fiat gearboxes, just like in Formula Panda. In fact, the only thing he changed was the bodywork, which was completely new — everything underneath remained Formula Panda. The cars had wings on the front and rear which really work: you can completely change the set-up of the car from understeer to oversteer by altering them.'

Hoecker bought one and built it. 'The problem facing me was that time was short — literally two weeks to the first race. I really can't remember how I first came across Michael and now, since he's made it big, everybody wants to know! Another problem was that I couldn't have a driver who was too tall — anyone of two metres wouldn't have fitted into the car. Michael was the right size (Schumacher was 1.74m; 5ft 7in).

'The decision wasn't made because time was so short, however. I wanted to win. I'd seen his promise in karts, I'd seen what I thought was potential. I rang him and he was delighted, he accepted immediately. He hadn't been in a single-seater race before but he took to it in a completely natural way and enjoyed success straight away. The car was right, the team was right and he was right. With hindsight, things look so different because at the time Formula Koenig could have been seen as insignificant.'

Aichinger expands on this, seeking its true context. 'Formula Koenig is not very far from karting. The cars are smaller than Formula Opel, smaller than Formula Renault, but you don't drive them exactly like a kart and it wouldn't be correct to say you do. It is, nevertheless, the perfect way to take your first step on to a real race track after karting.

'I began to know Michael then. I had not met him before. You have hundreds of karters but you never know how good they might be in single-seaters. In the first race, he did look good. He started in a good team and they tested and so on, so he was well-prepared. He won that first race (at Hockenheim) and he looked natural, he could drive easily, yes, yes, yes. Michael always looked completely natural. I think this feeling for a car is something you are born with, but Michael is fortunate in that he has the ability to learn very, very quickly. He's like a sponge, you know, he soaks everything up.'

Hockenheim wasn't easy and wasn't a smooth progression to victory. Hoecker remembers that 'Michael's gear lever broke during the first few laps — the race over 20 — and he could only engage gear with what was left of the lever. In doing that he hurt the palm of his hand.' A driver called R. Koester finished first in 26m 36.17s, Schumacher second in 26m 39.39s, but Koester was disqualified and so was Helmut Schwitalla, third.

'The first three cars were tested for legality,' Hoecker says, 'and as far as I can remember the disqualifications were because the valve

Right *Schumacher as he was when he came into single-seater racing.* (Werner Aichinger)

setting of their engines was not within the regulations.'

Aichinger, seeking the context again, says 'there were 10 rounds and Michael won them all except Zolder, where he had a little technical problem and finished second. The name of the guy who beat him at Zolder was Andreas Baier, who drives a Porsche these days'. Baier won it in 24m 58.42, Schumacher finishing in 25m 07.07 (which represents average speeds of 122.790kph/76.300mph and 121.623kph/75.575mph respectively).

'To win nine of the 10 rounds was absolutely outstanding and since 1988 nobody else has been able to repeat that, nobody. He actually won the Championship at Hockenheim (another round there, the ninth of the series) in a race I organised, and you should have seen how happy he was, absolutely happy. He hasn't changed at all, he's the same guy now as he was then, calm, very — how can I tell it to you? — well, you could talk to him about everything and if you asked him something you'd get a really intelligent answer. In that sense, it was the same as now, although of course now at a deeper level. He was never a guy who said "I am the greatest, I am a future Formula 1 champion". Never. And I noticed that he always did his best. He had the chance to do some Formula Ford 1600 races in the middle of the season and he took it. He was successful there, too.'

Thereby hangs a tale. Albert Hamper ran an FF1600 team. 'Schumacher's father rang me up and asked if I'd give his son a drive. His father said Michael was very, very good but the problem was that they didn't have any money. I said "no money, no drive!"' A tale of what might have been — like so many. 'Schumacher went to the EUFRA team, who gave him a drive without him having to pay.' Mind you, Schumacher's long-time mentor from Kerpen, Jurgen Dilke, had been active in raising some funds, as he had done when Schumacher was in karting.

Sieber remembers that 'Dilke was a good guy, almost like a second father to Michael. He said "you must learn English", and he taught him about racing. Really, Michael had no money of his own. He had an old Audi — his first car — and he slept in the truck. A real guy. We ran three drivers and Michael became friendly with one of them and in testing they'd practice slip-streaming on each other so they knew what it was about. You must remember that a Formula Ford car has no wings, no special tyres (one type, the same for everyone) but you can learn so much about setting a car up, about understanding it, about finding the right balance of the car. You have no real grip and it's easy to get too much understeer, too much oversteer and you have to understand these problems. Michael did.

'I said to him "once you get in front in a race you will always be a front-runner after that". He did it in, I think, the fourth race and he has been a front-runner ever since. We did 10 rounds of the German Championship and four rounds of the European Championship where we had a big fight with Mika Salo, and Michael finished second. You need a bit of luck, you know.'

'He was really quick, two or three seconds a lap quicker than anybody else'

In that Championship — the EFDA Formula Ford 1600 Euroseries, sponsored by Bridgestone — the Finn Salo was outstanding, winning four of the five rounds, although Schumacher didn't compete in the first, Zandvoort in June. Paradoxically the one round Schumacher did win — the last, also at Zandvoort — Salo didn't compete in. He didn't need to. He had the Championship already. This does not alter the fact that at moments Schumacher could push Salo: at the Osterreichring, Schumacher's Euroseries debut, he got to within 0.687 of a second at the end of the 10 laps.

One of the German FF 1600 races was at Salzburg. In retrospect this becomes pivotal. 'In practice we had our three cars in front, 1–2–3, but Michael wasn't that quick,' Sieber remembers. 'It would be a wet race — very, very wet — and I said to him "look, I can do an experiment on the car and if it works we win, if it doesn't we lose". Michael said "OK, Peter, do it and if I lose I'll go and have a beer!" He was nearly like a brother to me. If, say, the car broke down he'd say "forget it, we'll do better next time". At Salzburg Michael told me "everybody will go to the outside, I'll go to the inside. Plenty of space there". He got away sixth or seventh but he was really quick, two or three seconds a lap quicker than anybody else. He said "I looked in my mirrors and I couldn't see anybody behind me so I thought: now I'll drive with my head". He won by 20 seconds.'

Josef Kaufmann, a benevolent and wise Formula 3 practitioner as

Don't be deceived. Formula Koenig was serious. (Werner Aichinger)

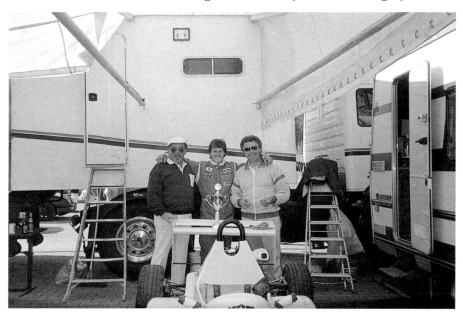

driver and now a team manager, watched fascinated. 'We'd done the Formula 3 race and then came the Formula Ford 1600. It was wet and I saw one of the drivers was fantastic but I didn't know him. I got a programme and looked and his name was Schumacher. I thought *there is one very, very good driver.* I can't remember if he won or came second but I do remember he didn't have a particularly good start. He ran sixth or seventh and worked his way up. To be able to do that is not normal with only a little Formula Ford experience. He'd only done a few races.'

Sieber remembers that afterwards Kaufmann 'came up and said "you can bring him into my team and you can come, too!"' A lot of people were talking about this drive, including Willi Weber, running a Formula 3 team . . .

That autumn, Schumacher contested the Formula Ford 1600 Festival at Brands Hatch, an annual gathering of dozens of youngsters from all over the place. The Festival carries prestige and produces plenty of action, some of it wild. Previewing the meeting, *Autosport* profiled 24 drivers, including Schumacher. 'Highly-rated by Jochen Mass, who wants him for the works Opel-Lotus team but has F3 aspirations.'

Schumacher went out in Heat 7. 'There was soon mayhem (behind the leaders) as Andrew Guye-Johnson and Schumacher collided at Graham Hill Bend, the local driver running wide over the grass, while the German retired with a wheel hanging off.' That was 30 October. The same day Ayrton Senna in a Marlboro McLaren Honda won his first World Championship at the Japanese Grand Prix Suzuka. In this one paragraph you have the two extremes of motor racing, the very bottom rung and the very top, and the interweaving to come.

That autumn, too, Weber, a driver for two decades and now running a team called WTS in Formula 3, offered Schumacher a test session at the Nurburgring. Kaufmann was there with 'my driver, Frank Biela. We'd done the German F3 Championship with him and he finished third but actually he'd had a chance to win it. At the Nurburgring, Biela went round and for five or six laps the Reynard of the WTS team followed him with, I thought, their regular driver Frank Engstler in it. Yes, I thought it was Engstler with the Alfa engine, though that seemed strange because Engstler wasn't that quick in Formula 3, always one and half, two seconds slower than Biela. I didn't know it was Schumacher driving the Reynard . . .

'Biela stopped and asked me "what times did I do?" We showed him the lap times and he said "these cannot be correct because Schumacher was constantly right behind me. How?" I said "well, your times are correct and because he was right behind you he must have been doing the same times". And that was the first time Schumacher had driven a Formula 3 car, you know. I couldn't believe what I was seeing. He didn't have any experience and he could stay with Biela.

'Like the Formula Ford at Salzburg, it was not normal that after only 10 or 15 laps in an F3 car you do the same times as a driver like Biela — and the times Biela did were good, Biela was habitually amongst the first three in the races and he led a European round against Morbidelli and the rest'.

Schumacher remembers 'after 20 laps I was faster than Engstler, I was faster by two seconds, so they made me sign a contract immediately'. Weber would become Schumacher's manager and mentor, forming a strong partnership. They'd contest German F3 in 1989 and Schumacher could bid farewell to Formula Koenig and those he'd raced in it.

'The car used by Michael in Formula Koenig is still in my possession, never driven by anyone else'

I quote from Formula Koenig's programme notes before the decisive Hockenheim race. 'The first year shows quite clearly that this "new blood" formula has a place in motor racing. It has established itself by finding Michael Schumacher and Helmut Schwitalla. That you can go straight from it to Formula Ford 1600 or the Opel Lotus Challenge is clear because Schumacher also won in Formula Ford.

'Only once has Schumacher been beaten in Formula Koenig, by the ex-mountain trials specialist Andy Baier when Baier raced like a man obsessed at Zolder. Schumacher's hardest opponent was the 24-year-old Schwitalla, also from kart racing, who was often rather wild at the beginning and sometimes had bad luck. Nevertheless he often got close to Schumacher and often enough finished only a few metres behind.

'Further drivers like Markus Hofmann, Kurt Gewinnus, Georg

Hutter, as well as racers from karting like Thomas Kracht and Thomas Gellerman, played themselves to the fore and made life difficult for fast talents like Frank Kremer or the powerfully advancing Detlef Schmalgemeier. That's how it should be. Because the regulations and controls are so tight, everyone has the same chance and success has to be won on the track. The mixture of drivers who form "Koenig's children" increases the attraction.'

A footnote from Hoecker. 'The car used by Michael in Formula Koenig is still in my possession and has never been driven by anyone else but Michael.' Schumacher adds his own touching footnote by judging Formula Koenig the 'ideal entry class' because it is comparatively inexpensive and rewards merit.

Formula 3 is a major step forward, and also highly competitive. In German F3, Kaufmann would run a driver called Michael Roppes, 'not at all bad but it was one of those years when you have a lot of good drivers. Schumacher was one of the best but Heinz-Harald Frentzen wasn't much slower, and you had Karl Wendlinger and Michael Bartels. All the season they were very close. Sometimes in F3 you get an outstanding driver in a poor year and he wins everything and you can't be sure how good he really is. Sometimes you get four or five guys who can really handle a racing car and even if you finish second or third it could be better than winning it in another year'.

Schumacher, Bartels and a driver called Frank Schmickler drove Reynards, Wendlinger a Ralt, while Frentzen began in a Dallara.

Schumacher demonstrated his speed in two 1989 pre-season races at Hockenheim. Race one: he qualified third, 2m 20.05s against Schmickler's pole of 2m 14.03 but finished a strong second, Schmickler 18m 32.31s, Schumacher 18m 32.59s — and fastest lap. Race two: he qualified on the second row and won. The Championship, over 12 rounds, would be harder. I'm indebted to *Autosport*'s correspondent Wolfgang Schattling for the words which bring the races alive because, as Schumacher says about doing so well so quickly in Formula 1, each race represented a gathering of experience.

Round 1, Hockenheim: front row, finishing third. 'Michael was immediately on the pace in F3,' Frentzen says.

Round 2, Nurburgring: third row, third. *Autosport* reported that 'the second round was deservedly won by Michael Bartels. The best start,

WIr machen
Formel 1
Sieger

— *AvD Formel König Youngster Cup 1994* —

Hockenheimring '88

Michael Schumacher: Sieger der Formel König-Meisterschaft 1988

m Nachwuchs eine Chance:

Unter diesem Motto treffen sich auch 1994 wieder rund 30 junge Fahr-rerinnen und Fahrer, um in die Fußstapfen des erfolgreichsten deut-schen Formel 1-Fahrers der letzten Jahrzehnte zu treten: Michael Schumacher hieß der erste Sieger einer Formel König-Meisterschaft im Jahre 1988. Von hier aus startete der junge Kerpener seinen kometen-haften Aufstieg über die Formel 3 und die Gruppe C in die Formel 1, wo er in Spa-Francorchamps 1992 erstmals einen Grand Prix gewinnen konnte.
Damit Michael Schumacher nicht der einzige siegreiche Formel 1 Pilot aus Deutschland bleibt, hat sich die AvD-Formel König zum Ziel gesetzt, diese konsequente Aufbauarbeit fortzusetzen.

AvD-Formel König-Teilnehmer in Action

however, was made by Victor Rosso, who came through from his sensational fourth grid position in his partly Russian financed Tark Aleco-Spiess. For eight laps the Argentinian managed to stay in the lead. At first he was followed by Frentzen, Schmickler, Bartels and Schumacher. Soon Frentzen's ill-handling Dallara was demoted to the back of this slip-streaming group and finally finished sixth.

'Bartels fought his way up to Rosso and outbraked him. He steadily pulled out his lead and came home more than three seconds ahead of a happy Rosso. Schmickler had an enormous high speed spin at the fifth-gear Veedol chicane when attacking Rosso on lap 10 (of 20). Although his Reynard was undamaged he could not get out of the wet grass, leaving third to Schumacher'.

Between the Nurburgring and the next round, the Avus circuit in Berlin, Schumacher wanted to take part in the Formula 3 support race at the Monaco Grand Prix but 'I was considered too inexperienced — and then the following year when I was in Group C (sportscars) I was told I wasn't allowed to drive because I had too much experience!'

Round 3, Avus, twin carriageways of autobahn linked by loops next to the East German border in West Berlin: third row, third. *Autosport* reported that 'Karl Wendlinger was the winner of a terrific slip-streaming battle. From the start, a group of six comprising Wolfgang Kaufmann (no relation to Josef), Schmickler, Schumacher, Frentzen, Frank Kramer and Wendlinger slip-streamed away from the rest of the field. The lead changed several times on every lap, with Kaufmann's Dallara and Frentzen's newly-acquired Reynard leading for most of the race. After poleman Schmickler had crashed out and Frentzen fallen back, a quartet consisting of Kramer, Wendlinger, Schumacher and Kaufmann remained to fight it out to the finish. They went into the last lap almost four abreast across the start-finish line. Wendlinger took the lead on the run to the last chicane . . . somehow the four-some made it through to the finish'.

'That was an exciting year,' Frentzen says. 'At the beginning it was difficult. I had an uncompetitive Dallara and my season only really began after I got the Reynard and became competitive.'

Round 4, Brunn: fourth row, fifth.

Left *Six years after he competed, Formula Koenig was still using Schumacher's name to show how good the formula was.* (Werner Aichinger)

Round 5, Zeltweg: pole, first, beating Frentzen (34m 57.803s against 35m 03.105s). Schumacher's pace 'spread the rest of the field'. A subtle undercurrent flowed at the lovely, pastoral Austrian circuit. Frentzen explains 'the ONS (Oberste Nationale Sportkommission, equivalent to the British RAC) backed both Michael and I and they promised that if either of us won this race we'd get a test drive in a Formula 1 car. We were both perfectly well aware of that so we had a hard battle. He had more speed and I needed to gain a tenth of a second in the Bosch Kurve (a spoon-shaped right-hander at the back of the circuit).

'The tenth enabled me to close up on him after the exit. I took the shorter inside line — there were only two lines, the inside and the outside because the middle was very slippery. Michael came from the outside, closer and closer, we banged and I spun off but I managed to finish second. That was the first time we'd crashed. Sometimes he was quicker than me, sometimes he wasn't, but we had a good relationship, fighting but always fair'.

Round 6, Hockenheim: front row, Wendlinger pole (2m 12.46s against 2m 12.59s) but Frentzen won from Wendlinger, Schumacher third. His consistency, however, gave him the Championship lead with 98 points, Wendlinger and Frentzen 83, Bartels 82.

Round 7, Wunstorf: the third row, twelfth on aggregate because heavy rain stopped it, the track partly flooded, and a second part was run later. Schumacher 105, Frentzen 103, Wendlinger 98.

Round 8, Hockenheim: second row and out on lap 10 of 14, the water hose failed. *Autosport* reported that 'pole position setter Frentzen made a blinding start followed by Schumacher . . . but Schumacher spun at the Ostkurve and had to call it a day later on with overheating'. Frentzen 121, Wendlinger 118, Schumacher 105.

Round 9, Diepholz, an anti-clockwise airfield circuit near Bremen: second row, fourth. 'Schumacher closed up on the leading group after a disastrous start. On lap 10 he was fifth and the following lap he outbraked Peter Zakowski to take fourth.' Frentzen 141, Wendlinger 134, Bartels 124, Schumacher 120.

Round 10, Nurburgring: third row, fifth. Frentzen 153, Wendlinger 152, Schumacher 135, Bartels 130.

Round 11, Nurburgring: pole, beating Kaufmann by almost 10 seconds. *Autosport* reported that 'Schumacher kept his Championship

Victory at Siegerland in 1988. The circuit was an aerodrome. (Werner Aichinger)

hopes alive with a lights-to-flag win. Championship protagonists Wendlinger, Frentzen and Bartels were involved in a first corner crash when Bartels pushed Frentzen from behind, sending him into a wild spin. Schumacher was in a secure lead after the first lap'.

Frentzen remembers the crash. 'I'd made a good start and gained two places, that is to say Schumacher led, then me, then Bartels, who came into the back of me and pushed me off. Going into the race I'd been leading the Championship too.' Wendlinger 164, Schumacher 154, Frentzen 153, Bartels 130 and out of it .

Round 12, Hockenheim, and a tight finish — only 10 of the 12 rounds counted, a driver dropping his lowest scores after that. It meant Wendlinger must finish higher than seventh to score points, Frentzen higher than eleventh, Schumacher higher than twelfth. But the permutations resolved themselves into a simplicity. If Wendlinger finished third he had the Championship regardless. Schumacher and Frentzen had to think in terms of winning and hoping. 'So we go to the last race,' Frentzen says, 'and Bartels has no chance of the

Championship. It had become a battle between Schumacher, Wendlinger and me. It was all a little bit nervous — Karl was certainly a little bit nervous. It was very difficult for him but we were all under different pressures.' Grid:

Frentzen	
1:01.61	Schumacher
Zakowski	1:01.62
1:01.77	Bartels
Werner	1:01.90
1:01.91	Wendlinger
	1:01.97

'I had the pole,' Frentzen says, 'and it was right for me because if the race finished in grid order I was Champion.' Bartels made the best start, reports *Autosport*. Frentzen, Schumacher, Zakowski, Marco Werner, Kaufmann and Wendlinger 'tucked in behind on the run to the first corner. When the long train of cars had entered the stadium section there was drama as Wendlinger had a coming together with Kaufmann. Both continued at the tail of the field. Up front Bartels and Frentzen were already in a race of their own, steadily pulling away from Schumacher, Zakowski and Werner. Frentzen desperately tried to get close enough to Bartels for a successful attack but every time he had put the nose of his Reynard under Bartels' wing, Bartels put some breathing space between himself and Frentzen'.

Frentzen remembers that. 'The race was on the small Hockenheim club circuit, very difficult to overtake. Bartels did make a fast start from the second row and I *had* to overtake. For a long, long time I tried but it proved impossible. I drove knowing that if I didn't overtake Bartels, Karl was champion.'

Autosport reported that 'in the meantime Wendlinger had charged through to ninth but then had another "off" trying to pass Kramer's Opel-powered Schubel Reynard. He had to settle for a minor placing (14th) which nonetheless secured him the title'.

Bartels	36m 55.00
Frentzen	36m 56.93
Schumacher	37m 07.41

This translated to Wendlinger 164, Frentzen and Schumacher 163.

'I'd lost the Championship but I had many plans that day,' Frentzen says, 'so I was motivated towards the next step of my career. I was disappointed of course but I was thinking only of the future.'

A hard season. Bartels says that the leading four didn't socialise because the racing was so serious. 'I won most races (three, the same as Frentzen; Wendlinger and Schumacher two) but I had the most crashes. We were all young, all a little crazy. We always drove with a knife in our mouth.'

(Amusing what-might-have-been. Albert Hamper wanted to run Schumacher at the FF1600 Festival at Brands Hatch. Schumacher wanted to drive in it 'but they wouldn't let him because he'd been in Formula 3 — so he never did drive for me, even once'.)

In November, Schumacher took the Reynard to Macau, a Formula 3 race of prestige run over two heats. Here he'd meet international competition, the ambitious among them eyeing Formula 1 itself, including McNish with a Ralt Mugen-Honda. 'This was the first time I'd raced against Schumacher since karts although, because I had raced him, I'd watched his career and his rise through Formula Koenig and German F3 when he finished joint second to Wendlinger.

'We'd do the qualifying and then he'd go off and play tennis for four or five hours'

'I can't remember speaking to him at Macau. To be honest, Macau was quite a different sort of event because I was racing with Theodore, we used separate garages and we stayed at Teddy Yipp's hotel. (Yipp, a benefactor of the event, had taken Theodore into Formula 1 in the 1980s.) We tended not to be with the other drivers at many stages.'

On the first day Schumacher qualified seventh, doing three hot laps and then plunging off. 'I like the circuit,' he said, 'but it's not easy. Next time I must wake up.' He improved to sixth next day.

In the first heat, McNish says, 'I was in it for a period of 100 yards or so. Otto Rensing crashed at the first corner.' A Swede, Rickard Rydell, struck Rensing, McNish struck Rydell, Eddie Irvine struck McNish and the crash rippled on back, the heat stopped. At the restart, Frentzen took the lead and forced out a 2.14 second gap to Paul Stewart by lap 1 before Schumacher took Stewart by diving past

The fruits of victory. Schumacher wins the 1988 Formula Koenig championship at Hockenheim. (Werner Aichinger)

him. Frentzen hit a wall but struggled forward, evidently 'delaying and blocking' as Schumacher tried to lap him. Later, David Brabham advanced on Schumacher who — and here is a glimpse of the future — increased his pace in a controlled way and won by 2.79 seconds. Schumacher led the second heat from Julian Bailey but Bailey took him. Schumacher drifted back and stopped with mechanical problems.

'Yes, I beat him at Macau,' Bailey says, 'and obviously he was good, but I remember two things. We'd do the qualifying and then he'd go off and play tennis for four or five hours, keep on until late at night for his fitness. He was the fittest then, and in Formula 1 he's the fittest now. As a driver he was on the limit and you could see the car was alive, the back end working. That is a sign of supreme confidence. Senna could do the same, dance a car round a circuit, you see Alesi do it. Others seem to have their cars on railway lines, which isn't the same thing.'

And that was 1989, Schumacher's career moving in an entirely orthodox way, step by step. In 1990 everything changed. The man in charge of Mercedes motorsport, Jochen Neerpasch, introduced a junior drivers scheme in the World Sportscar Championship, hiring Frentzen, Wendlinger and Schumacher to (in turn) partner the mature and experienced Jochen Mass. Neerpasch left undisturbed the partnership in their other car, Jean-Louis Schlesser and Mauro Baldi.

Classically, Schumacher ought to have gone to F3000, the last step before Formula 1. The World Sportscar Championship, called Group C, tended to be populated by three kinds of driver — the mature ones who'd done Formula 1 thank you, those never intending to go near Formula 1, and those who temporarily couldn't get into Formula 1.

Schumacher explored his reasoning at the time. 'The normal way is F3, F3000, F1, but it is not so easy to get a good car and a good team in F3000. My way is more safe. It's normal that only the top two drivers in F3000 get Formula 1 contracts, but I can win races for Mercedes, which is important, and get paid. Then maybe Mercedes will go into Formula 1.' Also, a second season in German F3 could be threaded in with the sportscar races.

Frentzen chose a variation, combining Group C with F3000. 'I already had the chance to do F3000 for Camel Germany. I'd the budget and the sponsors and I wanted to do it.'

Mass charts the background. 'I knew Michael before Group C, because at one stage I had an Opel Lotus team and I'd invited a number of drivers, he one of them. He refused it, saying "no way am I ready yet". He was in Formula Ford then. The Opel Lotus would have been something new for him, but he wouldn't do it because he didn't think he'd be able to do it justice. That's one of his strong points: he would not easily be persuaded to drive something in which he didn't feel comfortable. He was very open in admitting this was too fast for him. "I am not used to racing cars yet so I don't want to do it." I accepted that and I was impressed, absolutely. I thought it a very mature attitude. So we had Frentzen and Marco Werner, a German guy who did a lot of F3 and who was also very good. Anyway, that was the first time I'd had contact with Michael.

'Now, in Group C, I was given very little time to make up my mind whether I'd partner the three youngsters and it took me less than an hour to decide if I should do it or not. The idea was Neerpasch's. Mercedes took a big step in accommodating these youngsters. I was prepared to partner them — Schlesser didn't want to bother, Baldi didn't want to bother. I said "OK, I'll do it". I judged it would be interesting, I liked the kids anyway, and I had nothing particular to prove.

'If you're a kid and you come from F3 you want Formula 1 but you know that, to start with, it's out of the question unless you have a lot of money.' This does not mean sportscars need be a dead-end. They can be an alternative route although, as Mass says, 'nobody takes you to Formula 1 from sportscars because you are very quick. Something else needs to transpire: that you are *better*. Once, everyone scoffed at sportscar drivers and suddenly people realised that the drivers weren't that bad, suddenly people believed. That was the chance Michael took and he was wise to take it. He thought a works contract with Mercedes had some value behind it.

'They partnered me as it fitted into their other racing schedules. In the beginning the three were approximately the same although it took them different numbers of laps to get there. The easiest in was Frentzen, but Schumacher was the most analytical. Frentzen had an abundance of talent, probably more than the others, but his work capacity may not be the same as his analytical ability. I say may not. I don't want to beat him with a stick if he doesn't deserve it.

'He didn't make so many mistakes in German F3 and Schumacher

Schumacher at Macau, 1990, with reasons to be cheerful.

He and Mika Hakkinen crashed. Hakkinen walks back lost in sadness.

also made his few mistakes. What I'm saying is that one guy — Schumacher — is maybe more focused than the other guy, maybe he feels he has to work harder. That's just the way Schumacher is. Maybe it's a sub-conscious reaction to his feeling of his own ability. Schumacher was an extremely good learner and he makes decisions, which is another strong point, whether they are right or wrong — usually right but sometimes wrong. If they are wrong he admits it but he also learns from it and he stamps them out. He doesn't repeat them.

'I helped the kids but I didn't say *don't do that again*. I didn't need to do much of that sort of thing. Their own abilities pretty much enabled them to see through the problems and find the answers. I always helped. I was always very open with them because there was no reason to hide anything, and I never worked in a way of trying to gain an advantage by being a little more knowledgeable. I'd never deliberately have led them the wrong way. Actually it proved to be fun and you could see how these kids developed.'

'Schumacher was an extremely good learner and he makes decisions, which is another strong point'

Schumacher tested the Mercedes and 'sure, it had a lot more power than I was accustomed to but after six laps everything was all right. After 40 laps on the first test I was 0.2 of a second slower than Mass. The team was pleased. Frentzen was fast too'.

Dave Price, race engineer, attended the test at Paul Ricard and 'it was bloody cold. The youngsters came and I was a bit sceptical of Schumacher. He's going to get into a 700 horsepower machine which weighed three times as much as a Formula 3 car with three times as much power. He wasn't smooth, he was all over the kerbs, spinning it — ragged. But they have to be that if they are to get their act together, if they are to find out how to do it. You could see that he had something, however'.

Frentzen says 'we were immediately under pressure to beat each other because all three of us shared one car. Therefore, no excuses. It was like holding a hand of cards but everybody could see the hand, everybody could read the hand. The telemetry told everything so we could study each other very well. We knew why Michael was quicker on one day, I was quicker on another day and Karl was quicker on a different day. It was a bit difficult between three young men. Michael and I had a better relationship than either of us had with Karl, who was always a quiet guy. He didn't want to speak, he didn't trust so much, he kept it inside himself.

'Group C was a big test for me, a real test, that's right. The three of us were quick because we were pushing from the beginning, pushing each other. We were really motivated. You had to be quick without using too much fuel and that proved another challenge, that was more tension. You knew you had to be quick so you gave it everything in some corners, tried to save the fuel in others or save it on the straights. You try different tactics, think more about your line when you're driving in such a way and that proved a further challenge to us'.

Wendlinger, like Frentzen, didn't do German F3 but Otto Rensing returned to it. Josef Kaufmann says 'everybody thought, "now Schumacher looks good to win the Championship," but in the first race at Zolder he made a bad mistake and spun. He damaged the car. Maybe that was inexperience'.

Schumacher had taken pole after, as a contemporary account puts it, 'a handful of laps, and then sat contented in the pits'. He made a 'peach' of a start to the race. *Autosport* reported that he was 'well clear by the first corner, into the chicane. Rensing dived inside (Peter) Zakowski for second, only to have his wings run over. As Rensing slowed, the field bunched up behind, and Schumacher and the undamaged Zakowski were more than five seconds clear of the pack by the end of the first lap.

'By lap 7 Schumacher was a clear six seconds ahead and looked totally unbeatable but going into Turn 2 the car understeered into the tyres and his race was run. Schumacher made his way back to the pits on foot, to be met by his Mercedes sportscar team mate Jochen Mass. On the outside he kept his disappointment well hidden but he will obviously rue throwing away such a comfortable lead'. Wolfgang Kaufmann won, Rensing ninth after a pit-stop for repairs.

'I focused just on Michael during the season because he was the one to beat and nobody else; and it was the same for him the other way round,' Rensing says. 'Sometimes it felt very funny for me because we had a good relationship, we did work-outs. At the circuits we raced for

Main picture *Schumacher keeps on and wins, damaged car and all.*
Inset *Victory at Macau.*

the Championship but away from them we did do things together and that was nice.

'He was a very high-level racing driver. He worked hard for it and he thought about racing all the time — as I did — but there were very few others like that. Michael thought about everything which could make him win. People said that about Senna as Senna grew up. Michael was exactly the same and, as I followed his career, I always said he was the one who would beat Senna.'

At Hockenheim, Schumacher took pole, Rensing on the fourth row. The race was stopped on the first lap when, in the wet, cars spun off like tops, Schumacher — leading — among them. He rotated over the kerbing and suffered minor damage, rejoining far back after a pit-stop. Rensing worked his way up and won, Schumacher was nineteenth.

At the Nurburgring, Schumacher started from the rear of the grid, the car penalised for being 1.8kg underweight. He finished fifth after lively duelling which might have taken him to third; Rensing was second.

'I made a good start to the season,' Rensing says, 'but then I had problems, real problems, technical problems. I was in the lead at the Avus (the round after Hockenheim) and I fell off and Michael won. I took pole but it was tight (Rensing 1m 33.00s, Schumacher 1m 33.04). I led, Michael running third and my ignition failed: a part which in England would cost 50p.'

Two weeks after the Avus, Schumacher ought to have made his sportscar debut at the Sportscar World Championship at Silverstone, partnering Mass. In the Saturday untimed session Schumacher was travelling along the start-finish straight when the gearshift broke as he change into fifth. He parked it on the infield by Copse, the mechanics sprinted there and did hasty repairs. Schumacher 'rammed' it into third and circled to the pits. Officials excluded the car from the race for work done 'outside the pits' and excluded Schumacher for circling with his seatbelts undone.

Schumacher offered untypically vehement views about that. 'They say I don't have seatbelts, but I get into the car, start it, close the door, and then I close the seatbelts. Then I come to the pits and before I stop the car I open my seatbelts, and then I open the door, and the guy can only see that the seatbelts are open then.'

In German F3 at Wunstorf Schumacher took pole, Rensing on the fifth row, and Schumacher won from Rensing. 'We couldn't work out exactly what the problem with my car was,' Rensing says, 'but it happened again here. I didn't fall off but the ignition didn't work properly either.'

Schumacher made his sportscar debut at Dijon, he and Mass qualifying on the second row. Mass says 'I remember clearly that first year at Dijon. In a Mercedes C11 the track was a difficult one and the car not particularly comfortable to drive. They were finicky. He was a bit slower than I was — maybe I was in better shape or stronger and I could manhandle the car more — but I could see how he was coming along'.

A hot raceday and the track offered little grip. Schumacher circled nicely at racing pace not using too much fuel so that, after leading for three laps, he pitted and handed the car over to Mass with fuel to spare — so much so that Mass was able to turn up the turbo boost in the run for home. Schlesser and Baldi won, Mass and Schumacher under four seconds behind them after the 127 laps.

It was only when I was 20 that I said "hey, maybe this is what you do for a living"

Reflecting, Schumacher says 'it was only when I was 20 and went to Mercedes in their young driver squad that I said "hey, maybe this is what you do for a living".'

At the Norisring in German F3, Rensing took pole, Schumacher second row, and Rensing beat him, 39m 16.30s against 39m 23.48s; at Zeltweg Schumacher took pole, Rensing sixth row. Schumacher won, Rensing sixth. 'It was very bumpy,' Rensing says. Schumacher won Diepholz, Rensing third; Schumacher won the Nurburgring from Rensing (30m 55.99s against 30m 59.06s). Schumacher 123 points, Rensing 105.

Schumacher drove the Mercedes at the SWC at Nurburgring, although Mass put in the quick lap for a place on the front row alongside Schlesser and Baldi. In second qualifying *Autosport* reported that Schumacher went out on intermediate tyres 'just as the incessant drizzle turned to hard rain. On the first lap he lost it at the right-hander

Main picture *The Merc in action at Dijon 1990, where Schumacher impressed Jochen Mass so much.*

Inset *Schumacher with Jochen Neerpasch who created the Mercedes 'junior' team in the World Sportscar Championship.*

onto the fast sweeps behind the pits. The car pirouetted across the wet grass and thumped the barrier hard, with front and rear. Along the pit lane there were a few references to the junior team concept, but it was the first slip-up made by any of the talented threesome this year'.

Schumacher admitted the mistake. 'I pushed a little bit too much on the gas and I couldn't hold the car. There was a lot of damage.' In the race he and Mass ran strongly to be second.

The next German F3 race was at . . . the Nurburgring where Schumacher could take the Championship. Qualifying:

Schumacher   Rensing
1m 36.63   1m 37.70

A wet afternoon. Schumacher led, but at the first corner he and Rensing touched. 'That put Michael in the mid-field,' Rensing says, 'but in the corner after that I spun because my front wing was bent. I had to let the whole field go past. I really "started" from the back. I knew that if I finished in front of Michael the Championship stayed open, if he stayed in front of me he won it.'

A struggle developed at the front, Schumacher on a charge up to fourth and challenging Kaufmann for third, Kramer hard on Schumacher and taking him on lap 14 (of 23). At the right-hand corner before the pit straight on the second last lap Schumacher and Kaufmann tangled, but they kept on and hadn't lost any places. However, Rensing was up to fifth and because of the 'mayhem at the front' took Schumacher who counter-attacked, spun and finished fifth. Zakowski won from Kramer, then a gap to Kaufmann and Rensing. Subsequently Rensing was disqualified for reckless driving and overtaking under waved yellows. Schumacher had the championship.

Rensing says that 'it was very close and afterwards we had the drama. They disqualified me for something which never happened. They complained about my water gauge or something, they blamed me for running over a marshal but this marshal never appeared. Then they said "OK it was not a marshal but you passed under yellow flags". I still have the legal paperwork . . .'

Before the last round, Schumacher partnered Mass at the SWC in Mexico City. Late in the race it rained — Schumacher had done a blistering stint to take the lead — and Mass misjudged his pit-stop, tip-toeing round in 4m 17s to regain the pits. By then the lead had passed to Schlesser and Baldi, and Baldi brought the car safely home. Some 30 minutes later it was disqualified for a refuelling offence. At the last stop they'd taken on 246.1 litres: 0.1 over the allowance. Mass and Schumacher had won . . .

The German F3 season finished at Hockenheim. Among the entries:

M Hakkinen Marlboro West Surrey Racing Ralt RT34 Mugen

Hakkinen won. 'That was the joke,' says Dick Bennetts, who ran the team. 'We'd gone to Imola and beaten 42 Italians in their Formula 3, and Graham Bogle of Marlboro Switzerland jokingly said "I want you at Hockenheim and I want you to be across the finishing line before anyone else comes on to the pit straight".

'I want you to be across the finishing line before anyone else comes on to the pit straight'

'Why did we go to Italy? Marlboro asked us if we could. I think they were getting flak. They were spending money in England but questions were being asked about the amount when they couldn't advertise on the cars (due to British tobacco advertising regulations). Graham replied that the British Championships were the strongest and to prove that he paid us to do three rounds in Europe, at Imola, Hockenheim and the French at Dijon.

'At Imola Mika stuck it on pole and won by seven seconds, then we went to Hockenheim and suffered dreadful problems, a misfire in the first 30-minute practice — and we'd the wrong ratios because we hadn't been to Hockenheim before. It was embarrassing, British champions arriving at Hockenheim and something like twenty-second quickest. I remember someone coming up to me and saying "you Brits are not as good as you think, are you?"' Schumacher compounded that by going quickest.

'In first qualifying we jumped to sixth, still with a slight misfire, still with the wrong ratios and the chassis not handling the best,' Bennetts says. 'Ovenight we took a long shot. We played around and got the gears right. We took all the electrics out of the spare car and put them into the race car. On the Saturday we sent Mika out with old tyres and he came round and gave us the thumbs-up — the misfire gone. He came into the pits and said "the gears are good, the chassis is good, so bung a new set of tyres on". He stuck it on pole by a second.'

Hakkinen 2m 08.35s, Schumacher 2m 09.36s, Rensing 2m 10.19s.

'We didn't know Schumacher at this stage except that he had just won the German Formula 3 Championship. We'd heard of him but we hadn't seen him. I didn't speak to him, no, not really. Schumacher had done the 2:09 so I said to Mika "just bring your tyres in gently for a lap". He did that and went for it and we couldn't believe 2:08. A blinding lap . . .'

At the start, Zakowski slotted into second place behind Hakkinen but fell back into Schumacher's clutches and Hakkinen hammered out such a lead that he reached the Stadium section — where the circuit uncoils between curved concrete grandstands before the start-finish line — 1.1 seconds before Schumacher. Rensing, who'd also overtaken Zakowski, ran third and took Schumacher on lap 3. You know what Schumacher did, don't you? Counter-attacked, re-took Rensing next lap. None of this interfered with Hakkinen's stately and solitary progress to a new lap record and a 5.3 second victory over Schumacher, hobbled by a slow puncture in the closing laps. Rensing had been deep in Schumacher's slipstream but a rear wing mounting broke.

'Schumacher struck me as a very, very fit man, a very sharp driver, mentally alert and a nice guy'

'I ran under Michael's gearbox (clinging close to him) and I did it with a broken rear wing,' Rensing says 'The last four laps I had no rear wing.' That was third place.

A footnote from Bennetts. 'We went on to Dijon and the French didn't want us to enter. They made life very difficult. They said "you haven't got a French driver". I said "well, I've been through your records and you have a Belgian driver and a Japanese driver. We have a Finnish driver. What do we have to do? This is an international event and we have been requested to do it by our sponsors". They said "you have to pay £2,500 to get your truck into the paddock". I said "we'll leave it outside and take the stuff in on a trolley". They said "no, no, no". I rang Marlboro in Switzerland and they said forget it, so we never did get the treble.'

The season culminated in Formula 3 races in Macau and Mount Fuji, Japan. Schumacher took his Reynard-Spiess VW and prepared to tackle Hakkinen again, not to mention Rensing — but Rensing hit a wall in qualifying, ending his meeting. Bennetts says 'because we had beaten Michael at Hockenheim, the story was that they were going to get us back at Macau'.

The qualifying was in two groups, Schumacher in the first, Hakkinen in the second. Schumacher did a 2m 22.00. 'I looked at my pit board and I couldn't believe the time. It didn't feel any quicker than the other laps and I didn't even get a tow.' Hakkinen countered with 2m 20.88. The race was in two heats.

'We stuck it on pole,' Bennetts says, 'and won the first heat. From memory, when Mika crossed the line to begin the last lap he was like four and a half seconds in front of Schumacher and then he backed off and only won by around two and a half seconds (Hakkinen 35: 44.07, Schumacher 35: 46.73). I gave him a bollocking for that. I said "why did you back off? The bigger the lead you take from heat one, the more of a cushion you have in heat two". "Ah," Mika said, "no problem." Typical Mika.'

Before the start of heat two Chinese dragons 'writhed and wriggled' on the grid to the beat of a drummer and firecrackers were set off. Firecrackers in the race, too. At the start Schumacher hounded Hakkinen hard and between R Bend and Reservoir (the fast return section) surged through into the lead like a 'slingshot'.

As the race unfolded, Hakkinen looked 'wild' at Fishermans and Reservoir and took the car dangerously close to the wall. Schumacher looked smooth. Hakkinen, however, was faster through the speed trap — readings taken at a specific point on the circuit — and the additional speed enabled him to squeeze Schumacher at each approach to the corner at the end of the straight.

'Mika made a mistake or he wasn't pushing, and Schumacher slip-streamed past him,' Bennetts says. 'I'd told him "as long as you sit within two and a half seconds of him you've won the race overall, don't take any risks". Apparently around the back he'd drop away to seven or eight car's lengths and then close up to Schumacher's gearbox. Schumacher told me this on the Monday after the race. He said "Mika was playing with me". They came past and Mika was sitting one and a half seconds away, a good, comfortable distance, not any

Main picture *The Merc at the Nurburgring 1990, where Mass and Schumacher finished second.*

Inset *The drivers arranged statically in Mexico, the final round of the 1990 World Sportscar Championship. Schumacher is in the middle of row three, Martin Brundle — his future Benetton partner — row two, second from left.*

risk with the two and a half second cushion.

'*Then* the gap started to come to 0.9 of a second, *then* 0.8 of a second, *then* 0.6 of a second and, with only one lap to go, Mika was like 0.2 — right on his gearbox. I thought Mika would sit there and cross the line directly behind Schumacher. *Then* we heard a huge shout from the crowd . . .'

Autosport reported that Hakkinen was 'closer than ever before to Schumacher's gearbox as they rounded the right-hand kink past the pits. *Then* he pulled out to the right, to jink past Schumacher but Schumacher moved right a fraction to block him and Hakkinen clipped the rear of the Reynard, his Ralt then spearing left into the barrier and spinning across the track to retirement. A cry of shock rent the air. No-one could believe what they had just witnessed. Hakkinen hopped from his car, then hurled his gloves at the ground in a display of titanic despair. Quite simply, he had cocked up.

'As a tearful Hakkinen wandered about in a daze, Schumacher whooped it up with the WTS Racing crew. "I think he was crazy," he grinned jubilantly. "Nobody takes anybody on the last lap. Not without a fight. I spent the whole race thinking he would win (overall) so I am even more delighted now".'

Bennetts says 'Schumacher struck me as a very, very fit man, a very sharp driver, mentally alert and a nice guy. We were talking and I wanted to get his side of the story and he said "of course I wasn't going to make it easy for Mika to pass me. It would have been good for him to finish second".'

Question. For a proud and confident young man to confess that the driver behind is so good he's playing with you stands as unusual, doesn't it? 'Yes,' Bennetts says, 'it does.'

Rensing judges that 'some people — how do you say it? — are lucky people, some people aren't lucky. Michael was lucky. I'll never forget him winning at Macau. I was in the hotel room watching the start of the second heat on TV and I said to someone "everyone talks of Hakkinen winning the race. He has the better car, he won the first heat by a distance but I bet Michael wins the race". It is a feeling, you know, a feeling about Michael. During the season I'd raced hard

Right *Victory for Mass and Schumacher in Mexico but only, it must be said, because Jean-Louis Schlesser and Mauro Baldi were disqualified.*

against him and early on I was in the lead, but he's so strong he does give you a feeling . . .'

Schumacher dominated Fuji. 'We wrote the car off at Macau,' Bennetts says, 'and we had to build a new one. It had to be flown to Fuji and built in a hurry. It wouldn't handle, of course, and Schumacher walked off with a £20,000 bonus for winning both races. From memory, that was the year Schumacher was lucky. Steve Robertson (a Brit in a Ralt-Spiess VW) had a misfire and could have won Fuji.' Robertson and Schumacher contested the lead until the misfire.

'When Michael won the German Formula 3 Championship,' Josef Kaufmann says, 'the Reynard really was not the best car — and he won at Macau and Fuji with it, too. I am sure that that car was not good. Right after Schumacher stopped driving it, you could see it was not good. I think all the victories he had, it was not the Reynard car, only Schumacher.'

'He was mature, experienced, a young guy in Formula 3 with an old head'

Reflecting on the season, Schumacher said that 'all the lessons I learned in karting I used when I went through Formula Koenig and Formula Ford 1600. I could use my experience not to slide too much and so on. It was the same in Formula 3 and when I went into the Mercedes school with sportscars. There I learned a lot, too, about power, G-forces and power-braking. I was a lot quicker after this again.

'I was not used to this until I went to Mercedes and afterwards when I went back to Formula 3 I felt I could brake as late as possible and still have the car under control. I was used to speeds by then and it felt good. Driving the Mercedes you get another style and you can use *some* of this in Formula 3. It helps a lot, especially for finding the feel of the car and for using the tyres in the best way.

'I find the power (of the Mercedes) normal. Sometimes the team thinks I'm mad because I come in and say the engine isn't working properly when it is really. The best time is when you can use the big boost. It is so much fun. Driving with Jochen, Jean-Louis and Mauro has been fun, too, because they are so funny but serious in the race. I learned also because I was working in a team which was in every respect like a Formula 1 team, a big team, the technology very advanced and the car quick; and there was pressure'.

Schattling, who covered German F3 for *Autosport*, reflects gently and perceptively. 'Could I see that he was outstanding? If you're talking about the 1989 season when he raced against Frentzen and Wendlinger, no, I couldn't. I saw good talent — he'd come straight from FF1600 and Koenig — but he didn't make a big impact that first year. I thought Frentzen was the quicker one despite the fact that he made more mistakes. Schumacher was more reliable. You knew that mostly he would finish in the top three.

'The second season, 1990, he was outstanding. He was mature, experienced, a young guy in Formula 3 with an old head. He knew what he wanted to do. If nothing happened (mechanical failure or an accident) he won the races. He learns quickly and he admits that. From 1989 to 1990 he'd gained a lot of experience and he used it. Once he has acquired the data he needs, he uses that to the best effect.

'He was a shy, introverted guy. I spoke to him at the races, for sure, and it wasn't difficult. If you approached him he was quite open, but he didn't come to you (in the sense that ambitious young drivers sometimes court journalists). He didn't make remarks except about what you'd asked him. He was very straightforward, he didn't get into discussions with you but told you his opinion and that was it.

'My first surprise was when I saw how quickly he went in the Group C car. He took a big step from Formula 3 into such a car, and he outclassed the old, experienced drivers like Jochen Mass, Schlesser — they were looking foolish — and even Baldi. Jochen accepted early that Michael was outstanding. To go to Group C is an extremely unusual step for a young driver, but Michael knew that with Mercedes he was on the right street, gaining all the experience you need in developing a car with the technicians.

'And it was the right street for him to develop quietly, not in the limelight of single-seater racing at the highest levels. The experience he gained from this helped him a lot in single-seater racing. He'd had a great opportunity to develop himself by driving these fast cars during the winter before he ever raced one. He had 5000 km of testing during the winter, most at the Paul Ricard circuit but also Jerez — testing, testing, testing.'

And learning, learning, learning.

· CHAPTER FOUR ·

Diary of a Daydream

IF YOU'VE WON a Formula 3 championship you don't stay to have another go. You move on. In the spring of 1991 Schumacher seemed to be moving full-time to Group C where Mercedes paired Mass with Schlesser, Schumacher with Wendlinger.

In the first race, Suzuka, *Autosport* reported that 'with his tyres going off, Karl headed for the pits on lap 21, signalling the start of the first round of pit-stops. Alas, a potentially good race fell apart in a matter of minutes. As Schumacher prepared to return in the C291, the fuel filter valve on the venting side failed to close properly, sending petrol onto the hot engine. There was a flash fire as the car left the pits, which grew more spectacular when Michael turned into the first corner, much to the consternation of spectators in the grandstand and the crew members viewing the pit TVs. Schumacher was urged to stop over the radio, and he pulled off with the rear well ablaze, having to encourage some tardy marshals to direct their extinguishers properly'.

In the next race, Monza, the engine let go after 20 laps; in the following race, Silverstone, they finished second to Teo Fabi and Derek Warwick (Jaguar); the race after that, Le Mans, they finished fifth — Schumacher setting fastest lap. These races are covered swiftly because Schumacher moved towards a frenetic six weeks which astonished motor racing. He drove — respectively — a Ralt-Mugen, the

Mercedes and two different Formula 1 cars. The career exploded. No other word will do. The fallout hurt some.

On 28 July Schumacher contested the Sugo All-Japan Formula 3000 race with the Ralt-Mugen. He had not driven an F3000 race before. He came second in his qualifying group and ran fifth in the race, needing time to get past Ukyo Katayama for fourth. He achieved this by overtaking Katayama on the *outside* at the first corner. A Swede, Thomas Danielsson, lay ahead and seemed able to hold Schumacher, but late in the race he suffered an engine misfire and, with the engine cutting out, Schumacher breezed into second with four laps to go. Ross Cheever, an American, won it, Schumacher more than 10 seconds distant.

'The race was crazy hard for me,' he said. 'It was the first time when I must give 100 per cent for myself — sometimes over 100 per cent. The car is not easy to drive. You have suddenly oversteer, suddenly understeer. The car is not really consistent.'

'Michael is like that, honest. He's a normal man, just a normal man with a big talent'

Shortly after, Mercedes tested at Diepholz. Josef Kaufmann says 'I spoke with Michael and I asked how it was, the race in Japan. He told me he finished second to Cheever. He said he'd had a very good chance to win but he couldn't overtake. He tried to overtake but he lost too much downforce, there were some extremely quick corners and he couldn't close up enough. Michael is like that, honest. He's a normal man, just a normal man with a big talent. If he won races he was happy and now when he wins Formula 1 races he is happy. He didn't change.'

Schumacher and Wendlinger contested the fifth round of the Sportscar World Championship at the Nurburgring. *Autosport* reported that 'Schumacher tried really hard to find a way by Baldi but he was to suffer from a problem which has blighted anyone who has chased a Peugeot this year. The 905, it seems, bears some resemblance to 007's Aston Martin, coating all followers with a screen full of Esso lubricant. Indeed, after just four laps, it became so bad that Michael had to dive in for a clean-up, losing fifth place and 40 seconds in the

Inset *Eddie Jordan at Spa, 1991, talking maybe about Schumacher making his Formula 1 debut for him.*

Main picture *Schumacher, astonishing everyone in qualifying at Spa.*

process. Schumacher ran strongly to regain the lost ground but it became academic when he pitted after 10 laps. It was a terminal engine fault caused by a failure in the throttle butterfly mechanism'.

Careful, knowing eyes watched Schumacher that day. They belonged to Eddie Jordan, then in the first season of running his own Formula 1 team, and nursing a problem. His driver Bertrand Gachot wouldn't be available for the Belgian Grand Prix at Spa a week after the Nurburgring. He'd had a disagreement with a London taxi driver, sprayed a canister of gas in his face and was headed for Her Majesty's Pleasure in Brixton jail.

Jordan is a talent-hunter of rare intuition and reasoning. 'At our second Grand Prix, Brazil, in 1991, I saw Willi Weber. I'd known him because we competed against each other in Formula 3 and I was always friendly with Gert Kramer, a Mercedes guy who spent some time telling me how fantastic this Schumacher was. I'd spoken to Dave Price, too. It was, and is, our theory always to have good information. What we do might seem daft but over years and years, drivers and drivers of note have come to the fore. Maybe one day I'll pick a complete wally and people will say "we must watch him, let's watch him" and he does turn out to be a wally, but at the moment if I sign someone people take notice.'

Price, who'd been at Mercedes, can't remember exactly where the conversation took place 'although it was probably in Spain because I've a place there and Eddie has a place there. "What's he like?" "Bloody good." The conversation would have been as simple as that. I've great respect for Eddie and how he goes racing, how he finds drivers and we talk a lot'.

I wondered if Schumacher's performance at Sugo in F3000 swayed Jordan? 'The Sugo thing? Michael was just a replacement there and he didn't do a particularly great job. That wasn't what turned me on to him. What had turned me on to him was what he'd done in Formula 3, his approach to racing, the way he went about things. I'd seen him in the Mercedes Junior Team. I'd spoken to Dave Price, I spoke to Neerpasch and that's how it went.' (At the Nurburgring, Jordan met Weber and Neerpasch and, as he said a little later, 'all the details were agreed' for Spa.)

'I'd always try and look at different angles but, of course, until then it was unknown that anyone would come into Formula 1 direct from a sportscar never having driven Formula 1 before. It was quite unusual to take someone direct out of Formula 3000 into Formula 1 (unless they'd done a lot of testing, say). Probably my closest friend in racing, Stefan Johansson, wanted the drive at Spa but, you know, in the history of Jordan we have always tried desperately to do something with the young drivers if they have passion and commitment and fire and absolute devotion to what they are trying to do. Following that theme we said "OK, we'll go with Schumacher".

'We had a test day at Silverstone on the Tuesday. He had a couple of little spins but you could see quality and I think it's not that difficult to spot the driver's approach in the car. It's the same with Rubens Barrichello now (1994), it was the same with a lot of our drivers. Go back to 1982 when Ayrton Senna drove our Formula 3 car, first time he'd driven one, and he was instantly on the pace. These guys have a certain presence, they know what's going on. When we got to Spa we chatted on the Thursday' — and, although accounts differ on what the document was, Schumacher signed. 'On the Friday he was quick straight away, and on the Saturday, and on the Sunday . . .'

'He had a couple of little spins but you could see quality'

(Schumacher describes the Silverstone test, run on the South circuit, like this: 'The first three laps were quite impressive — in the impression they made on me — but then it was normal. Sure it was something special, but not over-special'. These are significant words. If handling the car is an overwhelming, uncontrollable experience even the first time you try, you're already in trouble. If it's just an extension of what you've already done, albeit an extreme extension, you're in.)

In free practice at Spa on that Friday, Schumacher covered a couple of exploratory laps getting down to 2m 12.382; on his second run he covered six laps and got down to 1m 59.254; on his third run he covered five laps, warming up on the first and then:

1:59.511
1:59.265
1:58.318
1:57.333

The context of that is astonishing. *He was already faster than other drivers would be in the session, including a driver with as much experience as Thierry Boutsen — a Belgian who knew Spa intimately. Schumacher had never driven it before.*

On his fourth run he covered three laps, warming up on the first and then:

1:57.593
1:57.654

On his fifth run he covered two laps, warming up on the first and then:

1:55.322

The context of that is equally astonishing. It put him eleventh fastest *and in front of thrice World Champion Nelson Piquet.* Gerhard Berger, quickest of all in the Marlboro McLaren Honda, did 1:50.343.

To familiarise himself with the car and the circuit, Schumacher covered 26 laps in first qualifying, quicker and quicker and climaxing with 1:51.071 on the twenty fifth — provisionally eighth on the grid *and still in front of Piquet (1:53.371).*

'Eighth fastest in your first F1 qualifying session is quite an achievement'

Journalist Joe Saward wrote naughtily, 'Schumacher is not well known in F1. Even Eddie Jordan, that famous talent-spotter, seemed to be getting confused about his driver. "Where do you think Schneider will qualify then?" he asked on Thursday as he organised a sweepstake among British journalists on where Schumacher would qualify. In the end, everyone was wrong and, before long, clumps of German journalists were talking about "the best talent since Stefan Bellof". Eighth fastest in your first F1 qualifying session is quite an achievement, particularly if you have no real F1 experience and have never raced at Spa. As a result of Herr Schumacher, much of the other action on Friday was forgotten'.

Schumacher said 'on the Friday I never tried Eau Rouge flat. I nearly braked, and firstly I took it in fifth gear, and then sixth. That was a problem, to get used to a part of the circuit like this where you can do it flat, but without experience you do it slowly and then step by step. With my first set of qualifiers I was just on my lap when Eric van de Poele went off and practice was stopped. The second time, I tried with the same set of tyres and Prost blocked my lap. He was starting his quick lap. I braked at my limit but he braked a little bit too early for me and there were only two possibilities: crash into him or use the escape road. I thought it better to use it . . .

'On my second set of qualifiers the time was not at the limit, not 100 per cent, but maybe a really good 98 per cent. I liked to take it easy because I wanted to qualify the car and not more. I didn't want to take any risks'.

On the Saturday, Schumacher got down to 1:51.212 (Piquet 1:50.540), worth the fourth row of the grid. In the Sunday morning warm up, Schumacher went an astonishing fourth quickest.

Patrese	1:55.211
Mansell	1:55.392
Senna	1:56.752
Schumacher	1:56.986

In the race Schumacher jumped the start — only slightly and understandable in the circumstances — but he burned the clutch and retired without completing the lap. Monza lay two weeks distant and what might Schumacher do there in the Jordan? The answer will never be known and the whole affair must be approached with caution because Eddie Jordan murmurs that it remains sub judice. I'll confine myself to what was common knowledge at the time.

After Spa, Schumacher tested the car at Silverstone, again on the South circuit, and did a lap of 54.4, faster than *it* had achieved before. The team manager, Trevor Foster, said 'we were not running the optimum set-up for a really fast time so it was an impressive result'.

Because what followed is complex and occurring at racing speed, I set it out in chronological order, remembering that the Italian Grand Prix would be on Sunday, 8 September. Jordan described the backdrop. 'A full contract was presented to Schumacher and his advisers on the Monday before Spa, following a meeting at the Nurburgring Group C race between Willi Weber, Jochen Neerpasch and me. All the details were agreed. Jordan Grand Prix had two letters of intent

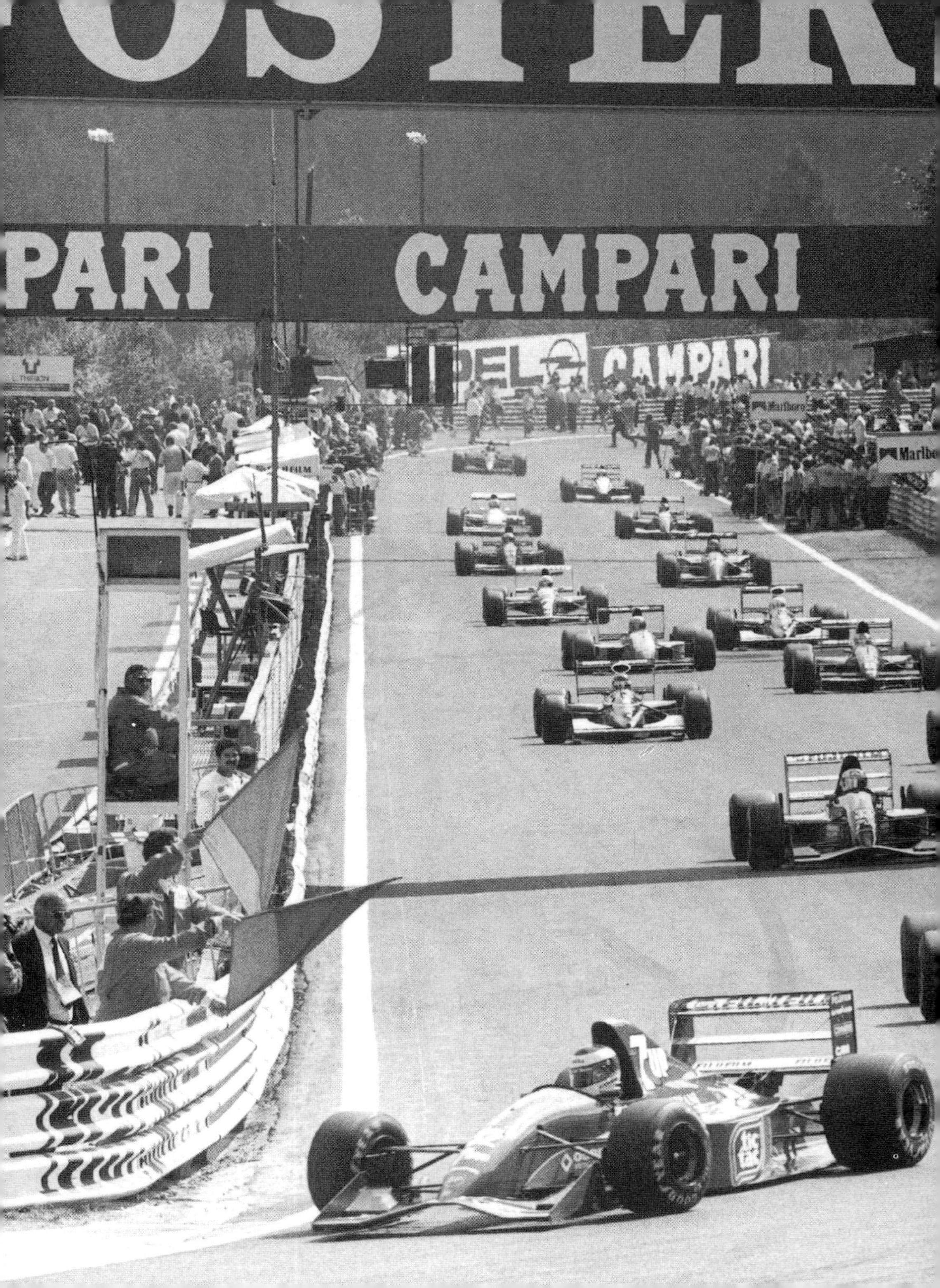
OSTER
PARI
CAMPARI
CAMPARI

Main picture *Spa and the warm-up lap, Schumacher rounding La Source hairpin. He'd barely get that far in the race . . .*

Inset *There were still the sportscars, of course. Here Schumacher chats to Bernie Ecclestone at Magny-Cours.*

from Schumacher, one in German and one in English, which were signed before the Belgian Grand Prix and confirmed the intention to sign a full contract with the team prior to the Italian Grand Prix at Monza. This contract was to cover the remainder of the 1991 season, 1992 and 1993. There was a buy-out clause in 1993, and in 1994 Mercedes had the first option for his services.

'During the week before the Belgian Grand Prix, Mercedes Benz Competitions Director Jochen Neerpasch confirmed to the Jordan team by telephone that he was in agreement with the conditions and terms of the contract. He added that he would be at Silverstone with Schumacher at 11am on Monday, 2 September, to sign the contract.'

At one point at Spa, Jordan had noticed 'Neerpasch take Schumacher off for talks with people from IMG and I wondered why?' (IMG are a powerful international company who manage leading sportspeople.)

Friday, 30 August. Neerpasch confirmed the meeting to Jordan's marketing man, Ian Phillips. Later, Neerpasch rang Eddie Jordan and asked if the meeting could be moved to London but Jordan had a second, unrelated meeting that day with Cosworth and declined to go to London.

The weekend of Saturday, 31 August to Sunday, 1 September. Neerpasch telephoned Tom Walkinshaw, the team manager of Benetton, and Walkinshaw remembered him asking 'whether we had any interest in Schumacher for 1992. I was surprised. I thought he was committed to Jordan so I said "if he's not committed then I am interested in talking". I wanted to try him in the car. It was decided that he would have a run and we would negotiate something or not based on that'. The run would be at Silverstone on the Wednesday.

Monday, 2 September, morning. Jordan waited at his factory opposite Silverstone and the clock ticked to 11am. Neerpasch didn't come and neither did Schumacher. 'He was at Benetton having a seat fitting,' Jordan said. 'When Jochen (Neerpasch) didn't turn up at the agreed time I'd chased round after him and had found him at IMG.' A further meeting was agreed, at the Jordan factory.

Monday, 5.40pm. The meeting began. 'When he (Neerpasch) turned up with Julian Jacoby from IMG instead of Michael and Willi, I was surprised and now I knew why. Michael wasn't allowed to attend. Neerpasch produced a contract and asked us to sign it. That was most unusual, because it is usually a team's contract that is signed, not a driver's. In any case, the contract was all in Michael's name and made him responsible for the money, not Mercedes. We could never have signed that as it stood. The IMG contract needed some amendments and I didn't have a lawyer present. I hadn't thought I'd need one. We agreed to reconvene at 10am the next day.'

Monday, evening. Walkinshaw had 'a phone call from them (Neerpasch, Jacoby) saying they had been at Jordan and had failed to reach terms. Would we be interested? We got together late on Monday evening'. They agreed to meet again on the morrow.

Tuesday, 3 September. At 'almost exactly' the time for the 10am meeting at the Jordan factory, Eddie Jordan said that 'a fax arrived from Neerpasch saying that negotiations with Jordan were at an end. Neerpasch did not turn up'. The fax informed Jordan that all Mercedes' guarantees for Schumacher's sponsorship and contract had been withdrawn. Jordan received another fax, this one a legal document which Schumacher had signed, which informed the team that he would not be driving for them.

The fax informed Jordan that all Mercedes' guarantees for Schumacher's sponsorship had been withdrawn

---

Walkinshaw and Neerpasch met. Walkinshaw said that it 'culminated in us making a heads of agreement subject to the confirmation that Schumacher was free in all the areas that I wanted'.

Tuesday, afternoon. Walkinshaw attended a meeting of Midlands businessmen and then flew in his helicopter to Silverstone to talk to Jordan. 'I told him what was going on. Needless to say he was a bit excited. I said "you must do whatever you think is right for you". I can only ask for all the guarantees (from Neerpasch) and I have to take those at face value. I cannot believe that a corporation like that (Mercedes) would make a statement to me that the guy was free if it wasn't the case. I signed him on the basis that he was free.'

Flavio Briatore, Benetton's Managing Director, met their number two driver, Roberto Moreno — who held a contract with the team to the end of the season — at Nice airport and fired him. Moreno decided to take recourse to the law 'to defend myself'.

Main picture *Two weeks after Spa, Schumacher had joined Benetton. He finished fifth. You ride the kerb this way . . .*

Inset *. . . then you ride it that way.*

Wednesday, 4 September. Schumacher tested the Benetton on the South circuit at Silverstone and in six laps got down to 54.6, after 30 down to 54.3, a fraction quicker than he'd done in the Jordan at his very first test. 'I was not surprised by his speed,' Walkinshaw said, 'but I thought he coped very well with all the pressure on him, in view of the fact that he's only 22.' Walkinshaw also said: 'Schumacher got in the car on Wednesday and we were happy with him. We signed on Wednesday afternoon'. He'd partner Piquet.

Thursday, 5 September. Jordan went to the High Court seeking an injunction to restrain Schumacher from driving for anybody else. It was refused. Walkinshaw said 'I had no problem with Eddie applying to the court. He tried on several counts and the judge dismissed every one. I think there's been a lot of nonsense on this. The fact is that the fellow, for whatever reason, had no contract with Jordan. He was a free agent. How anyone can allow a talent like that to be walking around the paddock I don't know. That's their business. When we were informed of that we went about the proper way of securing him'.

'How anyone can allow a talent like that to be walking around the paddock I don't know'

While Jordan's application for an injunction was being heard, the teams reached Monza for the Italian Grand Prix. Moreno defended himself by seeking an injunction in Milan that either he drove the second Benetton car or nobody did. It was upheld and the verdict reached the paddock at Monza at 6.30pm.

Someone described Moreno and Schumacher as 'tearful and confused'. Jordan said publicly 'I want to stress that I hold no grudge whatever against Michael, who is completely blameless in all this, and just doing what he's told'.

Friday, 6 September. Lawyers moved to and fro among the motorhomes until 2.30am when a compromise was hammered out, with the knowledge overhanging it that Jordan had obtained a waiver from FISA that they didn't have to nominate their second driver until 8am, no more than two hours before the opening untimed session. The compromise: Moreno secured $500,000 compensation from

Benetton for an agreement not to enforce his injunction, and Jordan got Moreno in place of Schumacher.

Neerpasch said, and natural justice demands that he be heard: 'Michael Schumacher signed an agreement with Eddie Jordan on the Thursday before Spa. It was an agreement to talk about an agreement. What he signed was a letter of intent. Eddie Jordan offered him the drive but he needed money. Mercedes-Benz agreed that money and asked for sponsor space. We talked with Eddie about the rest of the season and also the future, but only on condition that our money would guarantee a certain space on the car.

'I went to see Eddie Jordan on the Monday morning and we could not agree. A number of teams were interested in Michael and we went to Benetton. They wanted him and it is a straightforward deal. He is paid as a driver. I think the Jordan is a very good car for this year. There was no need to change. Michael wanted to stay with Jordan but Eddie would not agree with our requirements for sponsor space and wasn't prepared to discuss our contract. He wanted Michael to sign before Monza'.

Whatever his reluctance to speak now, Jordan permits himself to say 'I hope Michael realises what we did for him and I hope one day he'll recognise that publicly. That would be . . . the right thing to do. Write that if you like. Yes, write that'.

In that Friday untimed session, 6 September:

Schumacher (sixth)   1:23.662
Piquet (eleventh)   1:24.146

After qualifying, Schumacher was seventh, Piquet eighth and in the race he finished fifth, Piquet sixth. His local newspaper, the *Kolner Stadt-Anzeiger* hoisted this headline: MANSELL WINS BUT EVERY-ONE'S TALKING ABOUT SCHUMACHER. In Portugal he finished sixth (Piquet fifth) and at Autopolis, Japan, he and Wendlinger won the last round of the Sportscar Championship. In simple terms the end of the season comprised a sixth in the Spanish Grand Prix, a retirement in the Mercedes in Mexico City, a retirement in the Japanese Grand Prix, the win in the Mercedes at Autopolis, a retirement in the Australian Grand Prix.

A footnote from Maas. 'It only took the kids one year and after that they were on a par with me and then quicker than me. Did that upset me? No. What I thought and what I said was they have to be quicker if there is something there. They have to be. I was happy for them because if they'd been slower I'd have thought *jeez, they're not good enough.*'

They were, especially Michael Schumacher. He would now prepare for Benetton, his first full season of Formula 1 and the 16-race slog. Karts, Koenig and FF1600, F3, F3000, and sportscars were already curling photos in the drawer.

• CHAPTER FIVE •

Gathering Power

HE FLEW TO Johannesburg overnight suffering a minor irritation familiar to every long-distance passenger, 'someone next to me who seemed to have to get up and go for a walkabout nearly every two hours. That meant I did not get a lot of sleep.'

He spent a couple of days soaking up the sun, keeping fit and enjoying himself with his new team-mate, Martin Brundle, who'd joined from Brabham, Piquet having departed for IndyCars. 'Martin is probably not as keen on the water as I am, so it will be no surprise to learn that he took at least one unscheduled dip when he was not dressed for it — and I was! Of course, he tried to get his own back . . .'

The circuit of Kyalami had changed beyond recognition. The 'old', brandishing its fearsome, seemingly endless straight, lay among distant memories. The 'new' offered itself as custom-built in the modern style, but it demanded that the drivers become familiar with it. Hence an introductory session on the Thursday. 'I tried to spend at least two hours training on those days before we began driving. I liked to train at the same time of day as a qualifying session so my body gets used to it.'

Brundle, it seemed, could relaunch his career, and of Schumacher he'd say, 'He's ten years my junior and I wish I'd had his confidence at that age. He's a remarkable young man. He seems very fast but he hasn't got my experience. We're working well together because that's what Benetton needs, but I'll have my hands full beating him. We're going to be pushing each other along. He'll want to beat me as I want to beat him — badly — but that must be constructive, not destructive.' On Brundle a merciless weight of comparison would come.

On the Thursday Mansell made the Williams go decisively faster than Berger and Senna in the McLarens. Schumacher wasn't satisfied. 'We had a frustrating sort of day. The car felt very sensitive and lively, not the same as usual. Luckily the team were able to sort out the problem on Thursday night while Martin and I went out and enjoyed ourselves at the Heia Safari Ranch where the Zulu dancing was something special. We were both presented with Zulu spears! Willi [Weber] told me he had found a good use for it. He said he'd throw it after me when I came past the pits to make sure I was going fast enough.'

First qualifying settled (though we couldn't know it) the whole season.

Mansell	1:15.576
Berger	1:16.672
Senna	1:16.815
Patrese	1:17.571
Schumacher	1:18.251
Brundle	1:19.885 (17th)

'I felt physically good in spite of the heat and the altitude. I knew my training would pay off and that I was really fit. I do not like to do any jogging because it shakes up my knees. Instead I do a lot of bicycle work and build up stamina.'

At the green light Mansell made a fast start and Patrese sliced between the McLarens, leaving Schumacher to move on Alesi. Berger was travelling comparatively slowly and Alesi thrust by, Schumacher thrust by. Schumacher tracked Alesi lap after lap, but 'it's a track where passing is difficult'. The field stretched, Mansell clear of Patrese, Patrese clear of Senna, Alesi and Schumacher together. Schumacher took Alesi on the 39th lap and ran fourth to the end. 'My only other trouble [apart from overtaking Alesi] was with my rip-off visors. I accidentally pulled three off at once, and because Alesi's car was pumping out a lot of oil I found it difficult to see, but this is the best result of my short Formula 1 career.'

Schumacher, contemplating, 1992.

He'd been to Mexico 'twice before and I knew what to expect. The least said about my feelings for Mexico City the better.' The irritations of travel aren't confined to aeroplanes, either, whether you're a Formula 1 driver or not. 'I always stay at the Fiesta Americana Hotel near the airport. When I arrived I was given a room with the runways on one side and loud music on the other, so I had to change that straight away. Luckily I was able to get a quiet one. It makes all the difference to get a good night's sleep.'

In first qualifying only Mansell went quicker (1:16.346 against 1:17.554), and although Patrese accelerated in the second session it still left Schumacher on the second row of the grid, Brundle alongside. Schumacher had outqualified Senna (sixth) for the first time. That must be tempered against the knowledge that 18 minutes into first qualifying Senna crashed at the dreaded Peraltada corner, bruising his left leg and suffering shock. 'I had just gone on the track when it happened,' Schumacher says, 'and I saw it. In my opinion there is not enough run-off area and it is very dangerous because of the concrete wall.'

Here he follows Senna.

Senna recovered enough to do 16 laps in the second session, peaking at 1:18.791 while Schumacher improved to 1:17.292. Schumacher described the circuit as 'a challenge in a Formula 1 car. I like it in one way, because it is very different from all the others for the driver, but you have to watch very carefully and it is very bumpy. I found it was also very slippery because so much of the track had a new surface, and altogether it is a dangerous place to drive.'

No containing Mansell in the race, Patrese following, then Senna, Brundle and Schumacher. On lap 2 Schumacher took Brundle — 'Martin pushed hard at the start but then he disappeared [engine overheating] and I began to have trouble with my front right tyre, but as soon as Berger started pushing I found I was able to go quickly enough to control his pace.' Because Senna dropped out on lap 12 Schumacher found a clear run to third place and the podium.

In Brazil Senna qualified third, Schumacher fifth, and at the green light Schumacher went hard left to a vacant part of the track, tucking in behind the Williamses. Senna responded instantly in the first corner, the left. 'I really felt very cross in the race and my anger was directed at Ayrton Senna, the three times World Champion, and I will tell you why,' Schumacher said. 'I'd made a really good start and got ahead of him but he came round the outside of me [they almost nudged] at the first corner. After that I was quicker, but even though he was slower than me he chose to play around and I don't know what sort of game he thought he was playing. He braked in the slow corners where I could not overtake and then on the straight he accelerated and drove away. I was upset. I did not expect it from a three-times World Champion and it was not necessary.'

Schumacher spoke these words at the time and was perhaps not aware that Senna drove like that for a reason. 'During the early stages of the race,' Senna said, 'my car suffered a serious and intermittent engine cut-out. The effect of this was totally unpredictable and could occur four or five times on one lap and or not at all on the next. At times the cut-out was so bad that it felt as if I had applied the brakes. I continued with this problem, trying to cover it in the hope that it would eventually go away.'

Senna had already waved to Schumacher, signalling *I'm in trouble*, waved while he 'waited for the cut-out to go away. I raised my arm to warn drivers behind of my problem. The cut-out did not go away and was the reason behind my retirement.'

You can easily miss the undercurrents — nothing to do with a little argy-bargy (physical and verbal) between a couple of drivers that could be replicated at almost any time anywhere, but the singular fact that Schumacher in his eighth race felt enough self-assurance to criticise the great Ayrton Senna da Silva. Few others dared, except those who held the shield of long experience. Schumacher could have been announcing *I fear no man, fear no reputation, I am what I am.*

Spain might have been nasty. Towards the end of first qualifying the Benetton snapped out of control approaching a right-hander. The back whipped round and the car went backwards off the circuit, lifted and rotated on the grey-gravel run-off area, ploughed into the wall shrouded in dust, struck the wall hard.

'I'd been trying different set-ups on my race car and T car in the morning and in the end I chose the spare. I preferred it. The problem arose when I tried to do one lap too many on the first set of tyres. My left rear blistered. We changed them over, putting the left on the right, for one more lap, but it was too much. The rear left blistered again, I lost it and the car spun. It was my fault and at least I walked away unhurt. The car was not able to be repaired. This was annoying for me because I am sure I could have gone quicker.' It's the way drivers think, how they reason.

With the Saturday washed out, Schumacher lined up alongside

Mansell (pole). At the green Mansell and Patrese moved away fast, Alesi sneaking in front of Schumacher into Turn One. A wet race — 'the track so slippery I just could not find any grip or get going in the early stages.' He pursued Alesi for seven laps and made his move, placing the Benetton inside at a right-hander, Alesi turning in so that they almost touched. Schumacher held on. Mansell ticked off fastest lap and shed Patrese by lap 16.

Patrese went on lap 20, braking for a slower car at the quick chicane, losing downforce through the chicane and thumping the wall. Schumacher trailed Mansell by 22 seconds on lap 21 but rain fell. By lap 34 Schumacher cut the lead to 15 seconds and kept on cutting until it reached 7.01. With 15 laps to go Schumacher loomed into view through the spray. 'I did not notice how near I got to Mansell until it was down below 5 seconds. I thought he must have spun or something but then he pulled away again, nothing I could do. I concentrated on finishing in the terrible conditions. During the last laps I tried to wave to get it stopped. It was a battle to try and stay on the circuit.' Senna did spin — twice — and 'the second time I just couldn't hold it'. Mansell beat Schumacher by 23.914 seconds.

'I am bound to make some mistakes, and I hope people understand that'

Imola caught Schumacher out, something he was completely candid about. 'I made a mistake in the race and I had to pay for it. My fault, nobody else's, that's all there was to it, but it bears out what I have been saying for a long time now about myself, and what people have been forgetting. I am only 23, I have driven in less than a dozen Grands Prix and I am still learning. I am bound to make some mistakes and I hope people understand that. It is no surprise to me, even though I try my best not to make them.

'All in all, Imola taught me quite a lot. Grip and tyre wear are critical factors, just like engines and brakes, because it is a technical circuit and a very tough one. I found that the car handled a lot better on some corners than others on the Friday and I felt disappointed not to be better than fourth [behind Mansell, Senna and Berger]. I suppose one of my most memorable moments came when I produced a

Ten year span. This is Schumacher in 1984 as German junior karting champion. (Werner Aichinger)

This is Schumacher at the Canadian Grand Prix, 1994.

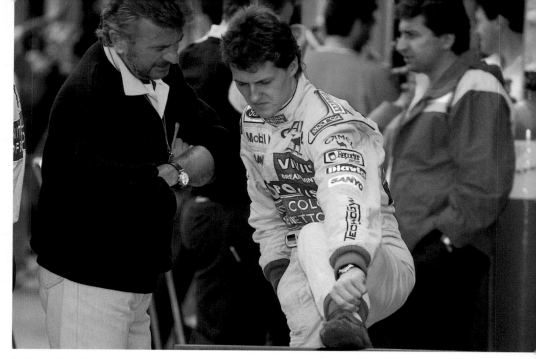

Left main picture *Schumacher in Jordan colours — very briefly.*

Left inset *In action in Formula Koenig, the next step up from karts.* (Werner Aichinger)

Above *Schumacher, listening and learning, 1991.*

Below *The team of '92, Schumacher and Brundle, and genuine smiles.*

Mexico '92, second race of the season and the first podium of Schumacher's F1 career.

The consummation of the victory at Spa, his first.

A dramatic embrace from girlfriend Corinna Betsch after Schumacher finishes second in Adelaide, '92.

Who said the glamour's gone from Formula 1?

Main picture *At the end of the season you relax.*

Inset *Schumacher and Corinna.*

Main picture *The hydraulics failed, spectacularly at Monaco, 1993.*

Insets *The car is winched to safety, Schumacher watches and then sets off at high speed — on foot.*

Victory in Portugal. Last minute team talk before the start.

The moment of victory, Portugal 1993.

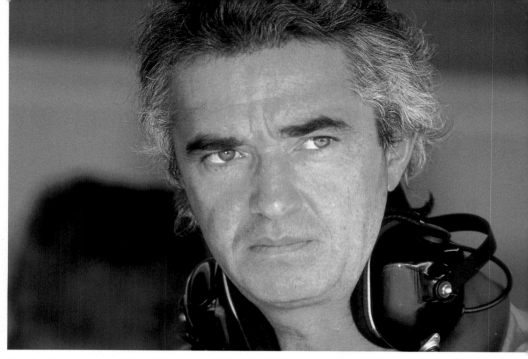

Flavio Briatore looking pensive, and in 1994 he'd have many reasons to look like that.

Senna and Schumacher, rivals, but for only a few weeks more.

Main picture *Nightmare in Germany. Schumacher's team-mate Jos Verstappen pits for fuel, some spilt and a fireball engulfed the driver, car and mechanics.*

Inset *Sometimes the strain shows.*

The 1994 Formula 1 World Champion is lifted onto the shoulders of the Benetton team. (Steve Etherington, Empics)

Brazil and a new season, new hope.

Imola 1995 and, on the grid, the drivers pay their respects to Senna's memory.
Schumacher leads at Imola — but he'd go off.

A rare quiet moment as '95 unfolded.

The response to all criticism, victory — and joy — in Spain.

complete 360-degree spin. I was trying too much.

'Saturday was even more difficult. We made various changes as we went along but none supplied the answers we were looking for in qualifying trim. At least I felt we were in good shape for the race. Martin made a good start and I was right with him on the opening laps when I made my mistake. I simply lost the car and it was damaged when I spun off.' The Benettons ran in tandem until Schumacher exited on lap 19.

Keke Rosberg, World Champion in 1982, is an acute observer of everything about Formula 1 and I rang him to ask for an evaluation of Schumacher. Did Schumacher show signs of immaturity at Imola? 'No, not just there. He has destroyed four Benettons up to now — I don't mean engines, I mean cars. That is immaturity, but what we have to agree on is that the guy is phenomenal. That he is also immature is only logical.

'I want to look at it the other way around and say some of his performances are incredibly mature, like Spain in the rain. Exactly. Bearing in mind the limited experience he has, to be immature is only natural and shouldn't surprise us. What does surprise me is how mature he is on occasions, in fact on several occasions.'

Brundle has said publicly that Schumacher is better now than Senna was at the same stage.

'Brundle has been talking about Senna now for the last 13 years. With all due respect to Martin, how can he compare them? Senna didn't start in a Benetton, did he? Senna was in a bloody Toleman, so you tell me how you can make the comparison? You cannot. Looking back over all my years, I judge that Schumacher is very good, but Villeneuve was very good very quickly. On the other hand, what I'd like to look at is who last got straight into a car which is capable of finishing in the top six all the time?

'OK, Villeneuve is the last one who did that, Alesi to a certain extent at Ferrari, but don't forget he had a season behind him with Tyrrell. But straight in with competitive machinery? Villeneuve. It didn't even happen to Prost, because McLaren had a miserable season in 1980. And if you do get a podium-finish car straight away as a young kid, you get self-confidence. In my day mechanics used to describe this as 'he thinks he can walk on water', and that's the phenomenon you're seeing now.

Nigel Mansell won Mexico from Riccardo Patrese and the podium was as happy a place as it traditionally is.

'Therefore I absolutely don't want to take anything away from Schumacher. He's looking very, very brilliant, but to whom do you compare him? Senna didn't have the machinery at the start, as I've said, and anyway he's a phenomenon. You have to remember his 60 pole positions in different cars, which nobody can take away from him. In Senna's case we were never impressed with his maturity, were we? He made a million mistakes at the beginning, but he was brilliantly quick.

'Schumacher often makes mistakes when they don't count except now at Imola where he made a mistake for which there is no excuse. Absolutely none. It was a bad, bad mistake. I hope the people around him will tell him that. He needs that to mature, to learn, to become even better. The problem with someone like Gilles, for instance, was that he was at Ferrari and when he went off nobody told him it was a mistake. The whole of Italy went *wow*. When he continued on three wheels [in the Dutch Grand Prix] they thought he was superhuman and that will never develop a racing driver.

'What Schumacher needed after Imola was a slap on the wrist. They should say, "My friend, you've now destroyed four chassis. In Barcelona you went off three times, in Imola you have spun during practice and you went off in the race."

'Mansell said very cleverly about a month ago in an interview — and I think it was very fitting — *the only thing Schumacher has to learn is how to drive slowly. Everything else he can do already.* And that's true.'

Your career was a struggle but you learned how to handle Formula 1.

'Age also comes into that, because he hasn't had time for the learning and it's difficult at that age to handle it all, isn't it? Tennis players probably have the same thing. You're into a big, big business and you're on top of it: big publicity, big pressures, big everything. I would say that all the responsibility rests in the first place with the individual himself, but secondly with the people around him in his management. We have to remember the international media is already saying that his feet have lifted off the ground. We've seen this in everybody, although probably less in Gilles than anybody else. His lift-off was only visible on the circuit. He was a really down-to-earth bloke who never walked three feet off the ground in the paddock, did he?

'Will the pressure swallow Schumacher? I had a similar discussion with Nigel Mansell a long time ago. I was very conscious that the biggest danger in racing — and I think Gilles taught me this lesson — is a kind of vanity. In '85 when I did that quick qualifying lap at Silverstone I was really mad with myself. I was mad with myself because it was totally unnecessary. OK, there was a goal, there was a 160-mile-an-hour barrier which I wanted to break for me. I wanted to demoralise the opposition, everything.

'In the same way I have to accept and understand Nigel on the Saturday at Imola last weekend and what he did in second qualifying [trying to beat his own provisional pole lap in first qualifying], but then you look at it from the other side: is it so necessary? He went off, he spun, he was on to every kerb. Why? He was already on pole by a second, one whole second. Anybody could have given him a written guarantee that he wasn't going to lose pole. At that stage what clever team management should have done is give him full tanks and start doing race testing.

'Anyway, what we discussed is that the biggest risk in Grand Prix racing is you get carried away. You lift off because you can get to a point where you believe you can do anything with the car — and you can't, it's going to bite you. That was a risk with Gilles in the

The start at Spa 1992. Senna, the two Williams, a Ferrari and . . .
Schumacher.

Master of the corners, master of the rain at Spa.

Getting ready.

The lucky mascot — a car, naturally.

beginning: he started by going off and then he learned to calm it a little bit. It was a huge risk with Alesi when he joined Ferrari, but that went fairly well because Prost was there to dampen him. It is a risk that we have with Schumacher now.

'You have to say about Michael that for his age and experience he performs very good interviews, he handles it well, but there's another pressure. More than any other country in Western Europe, Germany is so hungry for success because they haven't had it for ages, if ever. I hope this pressure doesn't push him too far. I come back to the point: find me another successful driver since Villeneuve who has destroyed four cars in seven races. The risk of injuries starts being at a very high level, and he's had spins on top of that. It's time to de-tune the performance just a touch. A 23-year-old is braver than a 35-year-old. Mind you, Nigel is bloody brave for his age, isn't he? He's good value. And Nigel knows how to look after himself, Nigel knows you can get hurt.'

Monaco would be a particular test because Schumacher hadn't driven there before and it's a tight, almost geometrical place, punishing error. In the free practice he covered 29 laps, exploring and discovering. He spun at the Loews hairpin, but might have been answering Rosberg because he — Schumacher — said, 'You find me a driver who can drive this track on the limit and not have any spins. It's that sort of place. I knew what to expect and that is why I came here early and spent a lot of time going around on a motorbike. I like to learn a circuit carefully, doing it in my own way. I am quite quick at doing this. I break the track down and learn it in sections. For Monaco I had five different parts to learn and I think I did a pretty good job with them.' He expressed disappointment that on this Thursday he hadn't qualified higher than sixth.

'Having a rest day on Friday [Monaco is unique in that the meeting starts on the Thursday, with Friday free for R and R and/or promotional activity] was good because we had time to work on the cars and I went off for a relaxing day. I went for a drive up the Corniche to see the Cote d'Azur with my manager and Corinna. We were so hungry we stopped for a hamburger in Nice! There we were on the French Riviera surrounded by so many great restaurants and we ate a burger, but at least it was a very good one.'

In the race Schumacher ran fifth behind Alesi for 28 laps before Alesi went, gearbox. 'I chased after Patrese but I had the same problem with him. I could only hope for a mistake but he didn't make any.' Schumacher finished fourth, 39.294 seconds behind the winner, Senna.

Schumacher hadn't driven Montreal before. He qualified fifth and ran fifth behind Berger. 'I felt much quicker but I couldn't pass him in traffic and when the fuel load went down he seemed to run a little quicker than me.' Senna, leading, went to lap 38 when the engine cut. Patrese went to lap 44 when he lost sixth gear, then fifth and fourth. Brundle had taken Schumacher. Order: Berger, Brundle, Schumacher. It lasted only a lap — Brundle's transmission failed, Berger 8 seconds ahead of Schumacher. The hunt was on.

'It makes me sad to upset people because I would like to give them some more'

Despite gear-change problems Berger stayed in the 1:22s, Schumacher matching that but not bettering it. 'As the race went on,' Schumacher said, 'I began to wonder about changing tyres but I didn't feel I had enough time in hand [over Alesi, third] so I stayed out to make sure of finishing second even though I had no grip.' He crossed the line 12.401 seconds after Berger. 'In the last ten laps I really didn't try to catch Gerhard because I wanted to finish second, and even if I'd got close I knew I wouldn't have been able to pass him.' Maybe he was learning the last trick: to drive fast slowly . . .

At the green light at Magny-Cours Patrese wrenched his Williams clear of Mansell, Berger third, Senna fourth, Schumacher hustling in fifth. 'I made a bad start,' Senna said. 'Gerhard and I ended up side by side at the first corner. It was close but OK. I followed him down the straight, he braked very late so I was being careful.' This was approaching the Adelaide hairpin, a hard right. Schumacher tried the inside and punted Senna. 'Schumacher came and hit me from behind,' Senna said. 'I think he totally misjudged his speed and his braking point for that corner, considering it was the first lap. He could not stop and hit me on the right rear.'

'I tried to go past in the last part of the braking area,' Schumacher said, 'but he came in and I could not/stop my car in time. We were very close and, almost inevitably, we touched. It was my fault. There was nothing I could do. I came in for repairs and rejoined.'

Rain fell, stopping the race after 20 laps, but at the positions on lap 18. By then Schumacher had set fastest lap. 'I have never been worried too much by driving in the wet.' At the restart, and at the Adelaide hairpin again, Schumacher and Modena collided, Schumacher briefly airborne. 'It was so tight. I tried to pass Modena on the outside because I thought he was going to the inside, but he didn't. He came across and we touched wheels and that was it. I went off and I could do nothing about it, but I can have no complaints. That is what happens in motor racing.'

At Silverstone 'the crowds are absolutely incredible and there were so many autograph hunters everywhere you went. If I were to go outside the motorhome I would not be able to move, and although I love to see people, it is very difficult because I have to concentrate on my driving. It does make me sorry that I have to upset people in this way because I would like to give them some more but sadly I cannot because of the pressures. There was no problem learning the track as I had raced on it before in the Mercedes, but it was a different experience in the Benetton, particularly the wind down Hangar straight.'

Schumacher qualified fourth on the Friday, falling back to seventh on the Saturday, but that was wet and the Friday times stood.

Mansell

Patrese

Senna

Schumacher

'There was some worry from the press that there would be problems between Senna and I following our crash at Magny-Cours because we were starting on the same row of the grid. Senna and I get on far better now than before the incident and I have learned a lot since then, especially that a race cannot be won on the first corner. My attempt on Senna could have worked, of course, and people would have said that I was a great star because I outbraked Senna — but sadly it didn't.'

The British Grand Prix belonged entirely to Mansell and the nationalistic engulfing: the crowd poured like a ragged conscript army on to the track with cars still going round. Who remembered Schumacher, fourth? 'The start was not too bad, but not good enough because Martin was quicker. I passed him at Becketts but I was going too fast and went into the gravel and then over a kerb. When I got close to Senna I lost downforce and locked my front wheels twice, but at least I didn't hit him. I stopped for tyres when I felt some vibrations and at the end I really felt I could pass Berger and I pushed hard. Luckily for me his engine blew on the last few corners and I passed him for fourth.'

Of the crowd invasion, Schumacher said, 'It was very dangerous. I was going flat out through to the start-finish line when I saw all the yellow flags. I thought there had been an accident off the circuit or something, then I saw all the people and I had to brake really hard. It was very frightening.'

Between Silverstone and the German Grand Prix, ten teams tested at Hockenheim, McLaren and Benetton among them. Senna felt Schumacher balked him at one point, Schumacher felt Senna balked *him* at another point. Senna journeyed to the Benetton pit and 'grabbed me by the collar — probably to give me a little message'. A couple of McLaren mechanics, sensing trouble, followed Senna and dragged him off.

'It was a simple misunderstanding on the circuit,' Schumacher said. 'In fact it happened twice. Once it was his misunderstanding and once it was mine. Afterwards he was very angry and he came to me and I was angry, too, but after a bit of a disagreement — it was almost a fight, but not quite — we were able to talk and sort it out. In my heart and my mind there is no problem between us any more.

'It all started after Brazil, really, and I was glad that after scrapping again we had time to sit down together and talk about it. I think our talk helped change his mind a bit and it also changed my mind. I don't want any more fights with anyone. People have suggested all sorts of things about my relationship with Ayrton simply because he made an impression on me when I was much younger. That, of course, was when I went to a kart race in Belgium where I saw him in action, and he really was very impressive, but it is not true in any way that I then said I wanted to follow his career and emulate him or anything like that. I never made him my idol or chose to copy him. I saw him driving his kart and never saw him again until I was driving in Formula 1.'

I fear no man, fear no reputation, I am what I am.

The power of the eyes.
The power of the eye.

Good moments, bad moments, 1992. Second place in Spain . . .

. . . but the long walk back after crashing at Magny-Cours.

He faced Hockenheim, his first German Grand Prix and rampant nationalism himself. 'I guess I was feeling a bit more pressure in the build-up because it was my home Grand Prix, but I don't think that this pressure has had any influence on my driving. One thing I have learned is that I need to have a better overview of all situations and to have a bit more control of everything in the job. It is in this that I am inexperienced and I need to learn.'

He qualified sixth and ran fifth behind Berger early on, although he rattled a kerb at the first chicane, putting two wheels over it and digging dust. The car bucked and twitched and 'I think I damaged the oil radiator'. On lap 14 his long pursuit of Berger brought reward. Berger pitted for tyres and the order became Mansell, Senna, Schumacher, Patrese. Patrese attacked hard, crowding, probing, Schumacher resisting. Patrese drew level once, twice, thrice, but Schumacher held steady and held him off.

On lap 33 Patrese did get through at the chicane. 'Three or four times I locked up the right front wheel when I was in passing situations with Riccardo,' Schumacher said when he'd caught his breath. 'We had a great battle, you know, and I think we both enjoyed it.' By 'passing situations', Schumacher means Patrese overtaking him! Patrese duelled with Senna but with a couple of laps to go spun off, opening the way for Schumacher to finish third. He hadn't expected that.

He reflected on his partnership with Brundle. 'In the last few races before Hockenheim I made a few mistakes, just as I said I would, but this was not due — as some people have said — to increased pressure from Martin. Where Martin is concerned I must say I do not feel particularly threatened or pressured in any way.

'I am still quicker than him in qualifying, but I have to admit that in racing Martin is fantastic. He is doing a great job but for some reason he cannot do what he is doing during a race in a qualifying session. I don't know why and I don't think he does. We have a good relationship and it has been even better since his successes in Magny-Cours and at Silverstone [third, third]. It has made things more equal, and he is more relaxed, as we both are.'

Hungary belonged to Mansell who, by coming second, won the World Championship. Schumacher ran fifth early on. 'I had been fighting with Martin for a few laps. I tried to go wide to overtake Gerhard Berger and I think Martin touched me. After that I lost my

Schumacher modelling,
Schumacher with model.

rear wing and I spun off.' That was lap 64, Schumacher third, and reaching towards the end of the long start-finish straight. The rear wing failed and was plucked violently into the air making the car undrivable. It rotated with a fury, smoke belching from all four wheels, skimmed on to the grass, belly-flopped across the gravel beyond the grass; and sank there.

Without labouring the point, Schumacher had now constructed a sequence — fourth, third, third, second, retired, fourth, second, retired, fourth, third, retired — on circuits that either he'd never seen before or had never driven a Formula 1 car round before — except Spain. In a sense, the run-in to the end of 1992 — Belgium, Italy, Portugal, Japan and Australia — would be at least familiar, and he liked Spa, anyway, although 'when I arrived I had a funny sort of feeling. It is a circuit I do not know terribly well, having driven there for the first time only when I made my debut. Just as 1991, I rode my bike to the track. I even stayed at the same place and tried to stick to a similar routine, but I had a very different feeling about everything. It was strange. I had a strong impression it might be one of those weekends for me. The feelings got stronger as the race came nearer and nearer. I don't know why. When I was in the motorhome before the race, I had it in my mind that I might have my first victory — and the first by a German since Jochen Mass in 1975 — but I hardly dared to think hard about it.'

He'd qualified third behind Mansell and Senna, but the logic suggested that Spa would embrace Mansell's Canon Williams Renault as eagerly as all the other circuits of 1992. The Belgian Grand Prix of 30 August proved a wonderful example of the illogical (and simultaneously Ayrton Senna's perception of the logical) as the weather taunted, teased and tantalised every driver.

Schumacher closed on Mansell in the Sunday morning warm-up: Mansell 1:55.409, Schumacher 1:56.571. In the motorhome Schumacher began to have the good feelings . . .

A dry start, but Berger's clutch failed on the line. In the jostle to La Source hairpin Alesi, behind Schumacher, took the inside, elbowing Schumacher to mid-track while Senna angled across Mansell. The order exiting La Source: Senna, Mansell, Patrese, Alesi, Schumacher. Out in the country Hakkinen (Lotus) pressed Schumacher who pressed Alesi — and took him. On lap 2 rain began, Mansell pressing

Senna, moving through on the inside in the Blanchimont loop, and soon enough Patrese moved by too. The Williamses were poised to give a demonstration run.

Mansell led the race and led the rush for wet tyres on lap 3, Schumacher in a lap later. Senna stayed out because 'gambling on staying out on slicks was my only chance'. Order at lap 6, the stops completed: Senna, Alesi, Mansell, Herbert, Patrese, Schumacher, Brundle. The rain fell harder, mist rising and gathering in the trees that hemmed the circuit. Alesi and Mansell nudged, letting Patrese into second place, Mansell third, Schumacher close in fourth. Senna's gamble failed and quickly, quickly, Mansell re-took Patrese, swallowed the gap to Senna. Mansell drew Patrese and both Benettons with him. Mansell flicked by Senna into the Bus Stop, the artificial 'chicane' before the start-finish line, and beyond Eau Rouge Patrese followed. Schumacher probed in the murk, Senna covering each move, but an inevitability hung over it. Schumacher went by, drawing Brundle with him. That was lap 13. Could Schumacher catch the Williamses?

'People had asked me about driving in the wet beforehand,' Schumacher said, 'and I thought back to Barcelona where I finished second behind Nigel Mansell in the heavy rain. Maybe I am lucky in the rain . . .'

He stalked Patrese and, as the rain stopped, the rush for dry tyres began, Schumacher pitting first. 'It was my decision to come in when the track was drying on the racing line. That was the most important part of the afternoon. It came after my only mistake [on lap 30] when I went wide and off at Stavelot. I missed the apex and when I turned in it was too late so I turned wide. I was lucky not to have an accident and go into the barrier. Martin got past me. I could see his tyres were blistered and that helped me make my decision to go immediately for new tyres.' Order at lap 31: Mansell, Patrese, Brundle, Schumacher — and only Schumacher on dries. 'Perfect timing,' Schumacher said. Brundle pitted that lap 31, Patrese on 32, Mansell on 33.

Schumacher's lap 32, at 1:59.824, was the fastest so far and it proved pivotal, Mansell still on wets, Schumacher now at racing speed and producing a difference of nearly 8 seconds. When Mansell did pit, Schumacher moved smoothly into the lead, and as Mansell worked towards racing speed himself the gap stood at 5.7 seconds beginning lap 35 of the 44. Lap 36 shaved the margin to 4.7 seconds. Schumacher

Fast food, 1993.

*Schumacher with Alain Prost —
talking about winning? You bet.*

*Schumacher in the unlikely role of
spectator.*

responded by breaking the lap record (1:54.760, although Senna, sixth, promptly beat that, 1:54.742). Mansell shaved the gap again, to 3.0 on lap 39. Schumacher responded by re-breaking the lap record (1:53.791), and now Mansell suffered an electrical problem, the gap suddenly yawning to 15.0, the race settled provided that Schumacher could complete it.

Winning your first race is a compound of many factors, not least mastering the realisation in the final few laps that you are going to win it. Schumacher controlled that absolutely, the car felt 'better and better' and he thundered Spa.

'My only regret, if I have one, is that my mother was not there. She was at home in Germany. It was very special, too, because not only is Spa the track where I began my Formula 1 career but the circuit nearest my home at Kerpen. It's only 100 kilometres, while Hockenheim is 250, so I always feel that Spa is like my home Grand Prix circuit. Perhaps that is why I felt so emotional. I could hardly believe it. I had tears in my eyes for the first time at Hockenheim, but I have to admit I really did cry after Spa.'

'In one year F1 can be so filled it is the same as five years for normal people!'

In the Italian Grand Prix, Schumacher charged . . . from last place. 'I made a terrible start with too much wheelspin and I had an accident on the opening lap when I touched the rear wheel of Thierry Boutsen's Ligier. It meant I had to make a pit-stop for a new nose at the end of the opening lap.' Lap 2: 25th. Lap 5: 22nd. Lap 6: 20th. Lap 7: 19th. Lap 8: 18th. Lap 9: 16th. Lap 11: 15th. Lap 12: 14th. Lap 13: 11th. Lap 14: 10th. Lap 15: ninth. Lap 18: seventh. Lap 19: sixth. Lap 27: fifth. Lap 42: fourth. Lap 50: third — where he finished, behind Senna and Brundle. It made him second in the Championship: Mansell 98, Schumacher 47, Patrese and Senna 46. In the background much unravelled, Mansell leaving Williams for IndyCars, Honda withdrawing — exercising a direct bearing on McLaren and Senna — Brundle to be replaced by Patrese at Benetton, Prost returning to Williams. It suggested that Prost would be the man to beat in 1993, Schumacher the man to beat him.

Two days before Estoril Schumacher went karting at Kerpen. 'That shows you how much I like it. It helps to keep me sharp and, contrary to many people's views, I think it is a really good thing to do. I often kart during the season.'

Estoril? 'The engine cut out, leaving me to start from the back of the grid. I also picked up a puncture and a damaged nose wing when I ran across debris left behind after Riccardo Patrese's accident.' [Patrese struck Berger's McLaren as Berger slowed for the pit lane entrance]. 'At that time I had climbed up to seventh but the pit-stop effectively ended my hopes of getting into the points.' He worked his way from tenth to seventh at the end, only the fourth time he hadn't been in the points across the 14 races thus far. The Japanese Grand Prix would be the fifth because the gearbox failed, but he moved to a strong second place in Australia behind Berger.

Of the season, Schumacher said, 'The hardest thing has not been on the track but off it. I have had to work very hard to get used to all the pressure, the people, the media, the television all the time. The driving is no problem, but the pressure increases. I feel I am getting more used to it and finding it better to cope with. The worrying point is that if I wanted to just sit alone in the paddock at a table in the sunshine to eat something, I would not be able to. I would have to disappear and that is something I don't like to do. I feel I want to relax at times but that is not possible — that is partly why I have moved to Monte Carlo. In one year Formula 1 can be so filled and so intensive it is more than the equivalent of five years for normal people!'

How do you put Schumacher's driving into context in 1992, even hearing echoes of Rosberg and a podium-finishing car immediately? I'll confine myself to the era that Rosberg's words covered. This is what the drivers achieved in their first full seasons:

	Team	Year	Races	Points	Best finish	Points finishes
Villeneuve	Ferrari	1978	16	17	1	4
Prost	Marlboro McLaren	1980	11	5	5	4
Mansell	Lotus	1981	13	8	3	3
Senna	Toleman	1984	14	13	2	6
Alesi	Tyrrell	1990	15	13	2	3
Schumacher	Benetton	1992	16	53	1	11

Accepting Rosberg's argument about the quality of the Benetton, you still have to do the races, bear the weight of expectation and deliver, and this at so many unfamiliar places. Great drivers tend not to tarry in securing their first victory. Villeneuve did it in Canada in 1978, his 19th race, Prost in France in 1981, his 19th, Senna in Portugal in 1985, his 16th. Mansell took until the European Grand Prix at Brands Hatch in 1985, his 72nd. Schumacher did it in 18, and as I write these words (April 1995) Alesi hasn't done it yet. Oh, and the merciless comparison: Schumacher third in the Championship with 53 points, Brundle sixth with 38, and leaving. I propose to let Brundle speak at length and allow his words to move into several inter-related areas.

'I realised he was an exceptional talent and that there was no point in blowing my brains out over it. Anyone would struggle to keep up with him. I have felt for some time that he is the fastest out there and, even before Senna died, I had become convinced that in terms of raw speed he was. He'd got his feet on the ground. He's refreshingly down to earth. He's got values, family values. He's close to his parents and does all he can to help his kid brother's racing. I've got a lot of time for him as a person and, as a driver, there is no limit to what he might achieve.

'I first met him in Group C when I was driving the Jaguar, but I didn't know him very well. The only real time we spoke was when I lost 10 minutes in the pits at Silverstone [in 1991 — a throttle cable broke]. I then drove back up through the field to finish third and I took three laps out of him. The other Jag won, he was second with Wendlinger, and I was third. I drove the whole race [rather than use a co-driver] and when I told Michael he said 'You drove the whole race?', thinking maybe he could do the same himself. And that was it, the only recollection I have.

'Unless you're a Senna or someone like that, you don't really pick your partner in Formula 1. The partner may be a stranger. What always surprises me is when you get chatting to someone like Mika Hakkinen and you discuss other drivers they'll say, 'Yes, well, when I raced against him in karts he did this and that, then when we got to Formula 3 he did this and that', and you realise some of these guys have known each other since they were 16 — because they've been racing against each other from that age. It's one aspect of being part-ners if they find themselves in a partnership. Whilst these people are not necessarily close to each other, they've known each other's driving

Pop star Paul Young seems to be making Schumacher apprehensive on a Ford Mondeo promotion day at Silverstone.

for a lot of years; but in the majority of cases you know very little about your partner other than his reputation. 'The relationship depends on the personalities and the chemistry and the contracts. Nothing revs you up more than when you can't get into the spare car because the other guy's got that in his contract, or if he starts getting the new bits, not you. It's a very competitive environment, and different people react in positive or negative ways. I enjoy a good relationship with my team-mates because I think that in Formula 1 you might as well work together up until the green light, but other people thrive on the aggravation. From what I understand, Senna used to ignore his team-mates and that created a problem for them in their heads, and then of course he was so incredibly quick, which created a bigger problem for them.'

The real tension is that the only person you can compare yourself with is your team-mate, because he has the same equipment. True . . .?

'Michael was quoted recently in a French magazine as saying, "I could outqualify Brundle" — he did, 16 meetings out of 16 — "but in the races it was different". I rattled him away from the start of the races and during the races, which has always been my strong point. There's no doubt about it: in the first four races of the season I had two mechanical failures and I made two driver errors, and the driver errors were forced because I had a team-mate who could pull laps out of the bag which I couldn't do. But he couldn't necessarily pull a whole race out of the bag.

'He was a bit immature at the time and it was, "Oh, I'm a young man and you're an old man" [Brundle 33]. He was very rude in the early days, but by mid-season I think he realised that he could learn a lot from me in many respects. We get on extremely well now and I think we got on well at the time once I'd come to terms with how fast he was. I hung on in there and worked on other aspects of my driving that I was good at. Benetton haven't found anybody since who could get remotely as near to him as I did.

'It's very difficult. Most drivers go trundling along in the belief that they are either the best in the world or potentially the best. If you are to achieve that goal, you have to believe it. Then suddenly one day you have to accept that someone is blowing your doors off [blowing you away]. Some people recover from that situation, as I did, and in the next 12 races after the mechanical failures and the errors I outperformed him.'

Brundle says that while some do recover from finding themselves pitted against a quicker driver, 'some other people just seem to collapse. It's a mind game. There are no bad drivers, there are no idiots, because you cannot drive those cars unless you are supremely skilled . . .'

Once upon a time the writer Eoin Young arrived after the start of a qualifying session and asked another writer, Denis Jenkinson, who was quick. 'They're all quick,' Jenkinson said. 'It's just that some are quicker than others.'

Martin Brundle chuckled when I recounted that to him, chuckled at the truth of it.

Approaching 1993, Schumacher felt 'much better mentally prepared. This is what comes from a full year's experience of Formula 1.' He felt the racing might be more open. 'Last year was quite boring, particularly for the spectators, with Nigel Mansell and Williams so far in front.' More open? Everybody mouths that incantation every new-born season, although when they mouth it most drivers are conforming to Oscar Wilde's description of a second marriage: a triumph of hope over experience. Not so in the case of Schumacher. The Championship itself did not seem beyond him, depending on Prost and the Williams and perhaps also depending on Prost's partner Damon Hill. McLaren had Ford engines (but not the state-of-the-art version in the Benettons) and Senna would only commit himself to the season race by race. Schumacher liked Patrese immediately, as so many others have, but on Patrese, like Brundle before him, a merciless weight of comparison would come.

A cameo of South Africa. Schumacher put the Benetton on the second row behind Prost and Senna, Patrese on row four. Senna led from Schumacher and Prost — Prost seeming in no particular hurry, a familiar tactic. Prost understood that races last a long time. He also

Schumacher's attention to detail, 1993.

understood that a 16-race season lasts a long time. Prost knew all about driving fast slowly.

He moved prudently up to Schumacher and on lap 13 went by. 'Alain was quicker than me down the straight so it was only fair to let him overtake.' Prost jousted with Senna and, given their past, it wasn't for spectators of a nervous disposition. Prost got through safely enough and so did Schumacher, who felt understandable elation at running second behind Prost. Not for long. Schumacher pitted at the same time as Senna, who emerged quicker. Across the next 26 laps Schumacher hunted Senna. 'I struggled to overtake him, but at one point I felt the time was right. I went on the inside, touched his wheels and spun off.'

A cameo of Brazil. 'I often find I cannot sleep at nights at tests, and sometimes at races, because my mind is running over the problems with the car. It was a little like that on Friday in Sao Paulo. I had been disappointed with our progress and woke up on Saturday with a new plan. It worked. Even Riccardo copied my set-up and we improved quite a bit.

'Fourth on the grid was not too bad and I felt pleased with my situation, particularly after I had passed Ayrton in the race [on lap 24 to take third place]. I did not want any further tangles with him after what happened in Brazil last year and at Kyalami, but then came the first pit-stop. To say it was not quite as good as I would have liked would be a massive understatement. The car fell off the jack, which meant it was left lying on the concrete and it needed two mechanics to lift it for the tyre change. If that was not bad enough, it was further complicated by problems in fixing the nut on the right front wheel.'

Schumacher emerged third but rain began and the pace car came out. 'I thought it was a good idea, but one which might have been timed a little more carefully. I'd have preferred to see it out a lap or two earlier when the track was very wet. My second pit-stop, to change back from wets to dries, was trouble-free, but not long after that I was brought in for a 10-second time penalty.

'To be perfectly honest I had no idea what it was for until long after the race when it was explained to me that I had overtaken someone while under a yellow flag. I was not the only driver to suffer for this and, since I believe I was passing back-markers at the time and they were easing off to allow me to lap them, I feel it was not the right decision. I know Ayrton had some very strong words to say about this [he'd been given 10 seconds on lap 24 for the same 'offence'] and I do agree with him. After that I did not think I had any chance of a podium finish or even the points, but I set about fighting back.'

With seven laps left Schumacher reached Johnny Herbert (Lotus) — third — and 'had a great scrap. I got past him once, he re-passed me and I nearly spun off on some dirt. He is a very fair driver. The next lap I tried again and this time he spun and I went through to third place.'

'He'll lean on you but he won't actually weave, or push you onto the grass'

'I saw him coming when he first caught me, yeah, yeah, yeah,' Herbert says. 'What did I think? If he wants to try up the inside or wherever, well, he can, but I'm not going to give him any room and if he takes me I'll try and take him back immediately. I don't like drivers who do mega-weaving and I'm not a weaver at all. If I'm going to be lapped I'll move over, but I'll always try and let them overtake at a place where I won't lose too much time. I'm still in the race, don't forget. If I can do a couple of corners with them behind I won't hold them up that badly and then I'll let them go.

'My thinking was: I'm going to get as tight as I can at the mid-corner so that at the exit I can re-take him. I lined that up before he tried to overtake because I knew he would try to overtake. You have to think like that beforehand. To the watcher it happens simultaneously, but I believe you drive a Formula 1 car with your brain working much quicker than it normally does. I know that after, say, a qualifying session when I'm driving home I can go round corners miles quicker without even thinking about it because my brain is working at the Formula 1 pace . . .

'Anyway, I did retake him and, ooooh yes, it was a great moment. I did nearly stop and cry [naughty chuckle]. It's a nice feeling to do that to someone like that and, in a way, you can laugh about it. *You don't get me that easy. Have another go.* You know he'll do it at some stage for sure. Michael is fair, he's not a weaver-weaver. He'll lean on you but he won't actually weave, and he won't give you the full push on to the grass.'

Inset *A familiar sight at the wet-dry-wet-dry European Grand Prix, Donington Park: the pit stop for tyres.*

Main picture *Schumacher in action at Donington before he spun off on lap 22.*

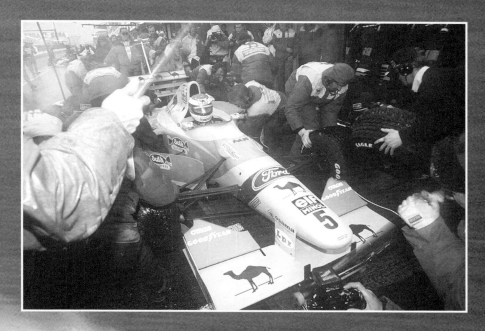

A cameo of the European Grand Prix, Donington. The race belonged entirely to Senna. Only Hill finished on the same lap. Schumacher rose briefly to fifth (twice) but 'when I was shifting down to third gear my wheel locked. I was running on slick tyres in wet conditions at the time, pushing right on the limit. I lost the car.'

A cameo of Imola. Schumacher's Friday qualifying time was taken from him because the team used 'evaluation' Goodyear tyres. 'I knew very little about this. I went off to play football in a charity match with a lot of other drivers. That was fun except I was kicked heavily on my left leg. By the time I arrived back at the paddock I was told my times had been disqualified. Neither I nor the team could believe it. All I'd done was use some B tyres, which I thought we were allowed to use. There was a lot of talking and the next day my time was re-instated. I was happy to see that FISA was big enough to admit a mistake and put it right.'

Schumacher put it right in second qualifying, third again. Heavy rain fell before the start of the race and he ran fourth having 'a great battle with some of the cars behind me'. That meant Berger (now Ferrari) and Wendlinger (Sauber), 'enjoyable because I know Karl so well since we'd been together at Mercedes. He was really pushing me at one stage.' [The interweaving theme from long past. Don't forget that Wendlinger also raced Schumacher in karts, but so briefly that Schumacher probably didn't remember.] Schumacher tracked Senna but Senna had a hydraulic failure. Prost won, beating Schumacher by 32.410 seconds.

At Imola McLaren put pressure on Ford to get the Series VII engines, or rather share them with Benetton. 'A lot has been said and written about this,' Schumacher said, 'and I have been mentioned in some places as saying that I would like to see Ayrton Senna have the same equipment as me. That is not what I have said. I only said that if it is in the team's best interests to have an agreement with McLaren I would be happy to race against Ayrton on equal terms. That is something different. I think it would be crazy just to give away something like that.' After Imola: Senna 26, Prost 24, Hill 12, Schumacher 10.

A cameo of Spain. He suffered 'terrible vibrations from the tyres from about half distance. This developed into a serious gearbox problem which went away when I changed tyres, but then came back with a vengeance later on. I could not use second gear properly.' He accom-

Schumacher led, and ought to have won, Monaco.

modated this problem and lapped in the 1:22s except lap 60 (of 65) when 'I came upon Zanardi as his engine blew. I could hardly see for the smoke and oil, but I knew he was still on the line so I pulled out wide to pass him. It was nearly impossible. There was so much dirt and gravel that when I turned the steering wheel the car went straight on over the gravel bed. I was happy to keep the car on the road after that to finish third.'

Schumacher had moved to Monaco in what he describes as 'a logical decision for business reasons. I had lost my normal lifestyle in Germany. When I was at home I didn't really feel I was at home. I had so much work to do and there were always interruptions and demands on me. I had nothing to lose by moving and Monaco was the obvious place. I could go out and relax properly at last. No one recognised me or made any fuss. 'In Monaco I am able to work much better on my conditioning than I would be in Germany, particularly during the winter. I am a regular at the Loews gymnasium and often work out there with friends or other drivers, particularly Aguri Suzuki. It was interesting to have the company of another driver in training. We did similar work, except he did a lot of running, I a lot on the bike. Mostly Corinna and I lead a pretty quiet life, as far as we can. It is home for us now, with all our things, each other and our dog. I am even in a friendly football team which meets to play regularly and I also play tennis and badminton.

'I went to play tennis and chose a quiet back court at the club. While I was waiting for my partner, I wandered over to see who was on the main court. Who else, of course, but Boris Becker? Surprisingly we had never met before, despite the fact that we both live in Monte Carlo. He said I should be down in the city going round the corners and I told him I was going to try his game out from now on. We had a chat over a drink afterwards but, as usual, didn't have enough time to get to know each other well. There is always other business calling, or testing, or public relations work . . .'

A cameo of Monaco. He got traction control and on the Saturday morning drove with and without it and estimated the difference as 1.2 seconds, specifically a best of 1:25.596 without, 1:22.209 with. He lined up on the front row alongside Prost who jumped the start and the subsequent stop-go penalty gave Schumacher the lead from Senna. By lap 32 he'd drawn that lead to 15 seconds, but at the Loews hairpin 'I think I had a failure on the active suspension system. I jumped out as it caught fire. There was smoke billowing everywhere and it looked quite spectacular.' It did.

He confessed he'd had 'a slight knee problem which has been affecting me for a few weeks now. I am not exactly sure what it is but it is sometimes quite painful. I notice it most when I am running or playing football. I think it may be a slight cartilage or ligament problem. It is not too serious but enough to worry me a little and I guess I will have to see a specialist.'

Before Canada, Schumacher had a five-day holiday in Nassau, then Florida. 'While in Nassau I even started reading a book, which is unheard of for me, and I completed it in one go. I quickly started

Main picture *Schumacher . . . the power that stunned the world.*

Inset *Schumacher leads, and holds off, Prost, Portugal 1993.*

another one and in two weeks I think I read more books than in the rest of my life! The books were called *The Company* and *The Judge* by John Grisham.

'After my break in Nassau — where the beaches were beautiful but the food not so good — I went to Orlando to visit Disney World. It was fantastic. We went to see the Magic Kingdom, but Riccardo told me afterwards that we missed some even better places to visit. Unfortunately the food in the Bahamas was a problem for me because it was entirely different from what I need for my conditioning and fitness routine. I could not get my work done in the gym after eating hot-dogs and cheeseburgers, so I was glad to get to Orlando. The first thing I wanted to do was go to a German place and eat some proper food, and with my food a shandy.

'I felt happy to have found somewhere like this, but the waiter, instead of taking my order, asked for my passport. I said 'Why?' He said you need to have a passport here to prove you are over 21 if you are ordering an alcoholic drink. I argued with him but I didn't have my passport with me. To make matters worse, the guy was German too! This upset me the most, I think. A typical German with his rules. So I didn't get my beer and had to ask for alcohol-free beer, but he would not let me have this either because, he said, it had one per cent of alcohol in it. I had apple juice with mineral water in the end.'

A cameo of Canada. The start 'went terribly wrong', a problem with the traction control adjustment. He nearly stalled twice, was briefly engulfed, both Ferraris through, and in the left-spoon-right corners after the start-finish straight Senna rode the kerbing inside and they ran side by side, wheels twitching together. Senna moved ahead. 'Obviously,' Schumacher said, 'I had a big fight on my hands to make up the lost ground.' He enjoyed himself, 'particularly the fight with Ayrton towards the end. Then on lap 63 quite suddenly he began to slow down, for a reason which I later learned was alternator failure. I don't think he could see me very well and we almost touched as I went around him at the entry to the hairpin.'

Senna said that 'the car suddenly started cutting out and I was so concerned about it that I didn't see Schumacher coming on the outside. I am sorry that we touched.'

Touched? Almost touched? Never mind.

Schumacher finished 14.527 seconds behind Prost.

Schumacher applies all the power he's consolidated.

A cameo of Magny-Cours. Running fourth behind Senna, Schumacher made a second pit-stop on lap 45 and set fastest lap two laps later. Senna said, 'I didn't change tyres for the second time because we felt it was best to wait and see what kind of pit-stop Schumacher might have. Had it been a slow one I'd have come in, but lack of power didn't allow me to go in, be overtaken and then try to get back in front of Schumacher.' Order: Prost, Hill, Senna, Schumacher, Brundle. By lap 58 Schumacher caught Senna and five laps later went by, Senna visibly slowing. The race ended like that.

Schumacher changed apartments in Monaco. 'I have just moved out of my old apartment to a new one which is bigger but still rented. I know you think we drivers all earn vast sums, but I don't have enough money to buy an apartment down there, I can tell you. In fact, if my landlady had not put up the rent when I was hoping to talk it down, I guess I might not have moved, but she increased it.'

'It was the best crowd I had ever seen — they were my motivation'

The knee problem recurred. 'Unfortunately it is no better than it was. It felt particularly bad at Magny-Cours because I went running twice. I tried to do a long distance on my bike in training [at Monte Carlo] but I really suffered afterwards. I went to a museum with Corinna and her parents but I couldn't stay. I felt I had the knees of an old man.'

A cameo of Silverstone. By now he regularly outqualified the McLarens and did so again, but on the Saturday went off at Copse, 'too much oversteer. I could handle it this morning but the wind direction changed this afternoon and the car just got away from me. I have to mention my team-mate and friend Riccardo Patrese. He was very generous and helpful. When I lost my car at Copse, I knew Riccardo would let me have his. I felt very motivated. I could not have gone any faster.' Patrese fashioned a best of 1:22.364, but in three laps near the end in the same car Schumacher probed then accelerated from 1:32.362 to 1:20.865 to 1:20.401. Hill led the race until his engine blew and Prost stroked the Williams home for his 50th victory, Schumacher 7.660 seconds behind.

A cameo of Hockenheim. He rode the clamour and might have had provisional pole, 1:39.640 against Prost's 1:39.046, but to hold Hill in the second session would be difficult and he couldn't. Just before the race he switched to the spare because the race car 'had been jumping around a bit and I did not know why'. Deep into the race Hill led, then Prost, then Schumacher. 'I did not think I had much chance of overtaking him and I knew the first set of new tyres, after the change, had been worth 2 or 3 seconds a lap. It was almost an ideal race. When I was running about 5 seconds behind Prost towards the end I thought about making a second stop for tyres and decided it was best to talk to the team first. We decided to change again. It did not quite work out properly and I heard a strange noise in the car over the final eight laps. That made me decide to ease off and change gear earlier to preserve the engine and gearbox.'

Hill went out on lap 43 when a tyre exploded so that Prost scooped up the Grand Prix, Schumacher slowing to 16.664 seconds behind. The crowd adored it. 'I was as delighted for the crowd as for myself because there were 148,000 there on Sunday. I thought it was the best crowd I had ever seen and they were my motivation all weekend. Some people ask me if the crowd and the media attention at your home Grand Prix builds up the pressure and makes life more difficult. For me it is not that way at all, although I did get a bit tired of being stuck in the traffic and crowded in by people every morning as I came into the circuit.

'In the last year, since I had my first taste of these big crowds at Hockenheim, I think I have mentally matured. I understand it all a lot better and I feel that everything in my own life is harmonious. I have no problems, no pressures, just motivations and ambitions. I knew the crowd was there to see a German driver do well and I did my best. I felt that my mental self, my physical self and my driver self were together in harmony. We held a press conference earlier in the week and had invited 95 German journalists. I was amazed when 150 turned up.'

A cameo of Hungary. Schumacher made a slow start and ran wide at Turn One, three cars going through. Out of Turn One into the short snap-right/snap-left Alesi moved inside. At the start of lap 2, Schumacher powered past Patrese at the end of the long straight and went for Berger, danced all over the back of him and at Turn One went outside, the car wobbling under the impetus. He caught that but almost immediately was on to the grass. 'After pushing hard I spun when the rear wheels locked up as I went down to second gear.' He churned the wheels and regained the track from a cloud of dust, tenth. Burn from the stern, but on lap 27 the fuel pump failed.

A cameo of Spa. He dismissed the fact that he was a second and a half slower than Prost, pole. 'We're quicker than McLaren and Ferrari,' he pointed out, 'and these are big names, but the Williams is the one we are measuring ourselves against.' At the green 'I released the clutch and the revs were not there. I had only 2,000 to 3,000, enough to keep the engine going but not much else. I tried to get the revs back up but I couldn't. It was like starting a road car in sixth gear, very difficult indeed.' As Prost, leading, reached La Source, Schumacher lay tenth. Burn from the stern. 'I stopped early for tyres,' Senna said, 'because I felt that would give me the best chance to fight with Schumacher.'

As Senna pitted — 7.11 seconds stationary — Schumacher passed, third. It had been 'especially difficult to get past Ayrton. He was a real problem. The team made a good decision to bring me in early [the lap before Senna] but I still found Senna difficult to pass and I thought he caused me some unnecessary problems. When I arrived at La Source after he came out of the pits he went straight out ahead of me and then to the left. I don't know why he did it. I nearly crashed into him and I would have done if I had not pulled right off and nearly on to the grass. It was not nice driving by him at all and I was not impressed.'

I fear no man, fear no reputation, I am what I am.

It settled Hill, Prost, Schumacher, settled to a lovely racing situation: Hill clear of Prost, Schumacher right on Prost. At Les Combes, a favourite overtaking place, Schumacher drew alongside, kept the power on, and as the right corner loomed he stabbed the brakes, brought smoke from the tyres. He was through. Could Schumacher catch Hill, 2.75 seconds ahead? No.

A cameo of Monza. 'We were never really in control at any time. The car was dancing badly, particularly over the bumps, on Friday and Saturday. At times I was really worried I was going to end up in the barriers, and at a place like Monza, where the average speed is around 150 mph, it is a pretty unattractive proposition. On top of all that I had a truly horrible cold with a fever which made me feel awful most of the time. It left me with no voice by Sunday morning.'

Senna and Hill bumped at the first chicane, making Schumacher

Right *It never seems a waste of champagne at the time.*

third. On lap 4 he took Alesi but around Monza's broad acres Prost drove into another dimension, far beyond reach, and Schumacher's engine went, 'a terrible noise from the back of the car just after I had left the first chicane'.

An extended cameo of Estoril. On the Friday Prost took provisional pole and called a Press Conference to announce his retirement.

Thus Schumacher's first qualifying — fifth — drowned in the jostle and rumble of Prost. Who noticed Hakkinen, who'd replaced the luckless Michael Andretti at McLaren? Moreover, Schumacher fell back to sixth in second qualifying. 'I was getting understeer, oversteer and bumping. We worked on it. I even copied Riccardo's software and settings on to my car because he seemed to be having a reasonable time, but none of it worked. I was pretty sure it was a computer problem with the active suspension system, but finding it and solving it was another matter.

'After Saturday I stayed at the circuit until 11 o'clock at night. It was a worrying time for myself and everyone in the team. I can honestly say I have never worked so hard at a race. I am known to be a hard worker and I am usually one of the last, if not the last, to leave the circuit, but this was worse than anything I had known.' He went to bed with 'data about the car swimming before my eyes. I had no idea that we would be able to solve the problems.'

In Sunday morning warm-up 'we were going slower and slower' and in the wrong direction. Hill, pole, covered 13 laps working down to 16.446 on his first run, 1:15.773 on his second. Schumacher covered 14 laps working down to 1:17.927 on his first, 1:17.750 on his second. He tried the race car and the spare and chose the spare. 'Frankly, we hoped for the best.'

Hill couldn't get away from the dummy grid and would start from the back, giving

(Vacant)
                    Prost
        Hakkinen
                    Senna
            Alesi
                    Schumacher

At the green Hakkinen moved urgently alongside Prost and by the mouth of Turn One Prost saw Hakkinen just ahead, Senna looking to dart past Hakkinen, Alesi over to the left. Alesi kept coming round the outside like a hammer and cumulatively it squeezed Prost to fourth, Schumacher three lengths distant. Schumacher went for him.

'It was one of those races where everyone was driving closely together from the start. You had to be careful and you had to conserve the car well and the tyres. To err on the side of caution we planned to make two pit-stops, but once the race started it was a different story. And what a start. Who would have expected Jean Alesi to be leading in the first corner?'

Answer: Jean Alesi.

Senna nipped out and took Hakkinen and that stayed the order for the first 19 laps, by which time Hill, burning, was sixth. 'I was trying

Power in Japan — but he collided with Damon Hill.

Straight-line speed in Japan.

to get past Prost in the early part, but I found it very difficult,' Schumacher said. 'The car was handling really well but we needed something else if we were to make up places. That is when I decided to come in and change my tyres early. It worked.'

Senna went on lap 19, engine, and at lap 23, Prost leading, the Hill-to-Schumacher gap stood at 7 seconds. A flash reading came up, Prost leading Hill by 15 seconds, Schumacher closing to within 4 seconds of Hill. In traffic Schumacher caught Hill, leaving him utterly vulnerable. Prost pitted on lap 29, was stationary for 6.82 and almost stalled; Hill pitted a lap later. Schumacher led.

'I suddenly found myself with a chance of winning *if I did not come in for the second scheduled pit-stop*. I don't think anyone in the team wanted to argue about me staying out. I did my best to look after the tyres from then on. I tried also to control the gap I had ahead of Prost and it was not easy. It went from 2 seconds out to 6 and then back again, and at the end of the race Alain was definitely quicker.'

'I'm sure I could have caught Senna and challenged him for the lead'

On lap 36 Prost did 1:16.322, fastest of the race and cutting the gap to 4.4. For Prost second place would be enough for the Championship. Would he settle for that? He cut the gap to 3.08, but they were in constant traffic and the gap went out to more than 7.0. Some 30 laps remained and few men on earth understood the possibilities of time better than Alain Prost. On lap 42 he did 1:16.386, fastest. Schumacher flowed up to the tail of a crocodile of four cars — Brundle, Patrese, Erik Comas (Larrousse) and J J Lehto (Sauber), Prost with a clear run at him.

Schumacher cut past Brundle and Patrese, Prost drawing up to them and cranking out a new fastest lap, 1:15.780. Schumacher sliced past Comas and rushed towards Lehto. Prost closed on Patrese, Schumacher captive behind Lehto although he tried to thrust inside. Lehto closed the door. On lap 49 Prost executed a classical overtaking move at the end of the start-finish straight: a tow, up tight, flick inside, goodbye. He might have done it from memory. In moments he'd be gazing at Schumacher — still behind Lehto.

Next lap on the start-finish straight Schumacher waved an arm at Lehto who stayed firmly in front. Schumacher swarmed, Prost lurking, watching, gauging, waiting. He had time. Suddenly Schumacher went full on to the power, shedding Lehto at last, but Prost did that too.

	Schumacher	*Prost*
Lap 52	1:16.729	1:16.987
Lap 53	1:16.768	1:16.663
Lap 54	1:16.549	1:16.207
Lap 55	1:16.255	1:16.071

The laps melted, each like the other, the cars equidistant. Schumacher lapped Philippe Alliott (Larrousse) but Prost couldn't immediately, giving Schumacher respite, but not much. Next time he glanced in the mirrors Prost was back. In those last few laps Schumacher resisted whatever pressure Prost laid on him and won by 0.982 of a second.

A cameo of Japan. He crashed. 'I was trying to stay close to Berger to stop Hill from moving inside, but he did and I hit his wheel. The impact knocked my wheel off.'

A cameo of Australia. He pitted early for tyres, but the engine let go shortly after. 'I'm sure I could have caught Senna [the winner] and maybe challenged him for the lead. It's a shame.'

I fear no man, fear no reputation, I am what I am.

Oh, and the merciless comparison: Schumacher fourth in the Championship with 52 points, Patrese fifth with 20 and leaving.

• CHAPTER SIX •

The Battered Crown

EVERYTHING SEEMED CLEAR as January turned into February and February turned into early March amid the usual winter testing, launching of new cars and triumphs of hope over experience: Senna at Canon Williams Renault to partner Hill, Lehto at Benetton to partner Schumacher. Lehto and Hill were regarded as supporting cast and either Senna or Schumacher would have the 1994 Championship. Surely. Senna had the envied car, Schumacher had the car nobody should underestimate.

On Lehto the merciless weight of comparison would come.

January turning gently into February, Formula 1 appeared as ordered as it can ever hope to be. An array of electronic driver aids had been banned to return the art of driving from the microchip to the human being. Who would handle the art form best?

Benetton unveiled the B194 early in January (which is early) and it would have Ford's new Zetec-R engine. At the unveiling someone asked Schumacher if Lehto would push him. 'I don't think I've ever needed motivation of that sort, because I've had Senna in front of me, which is great motivation.' He'd undergone an operation on his knees and 'they are fine. I can walk normally.'

At Silverstone in testing Lehto plunged off at Stowe and hit a tyre barrier. He needed surgery on his back and injured his neck.

At Barcelona in testing Hill did 1:18.2 against Schumacher's 1:18.9, but that was the Monday. Later Schumacher did 1:17.60, which, as everyone noted, was faster than Prost's 1993 pole of 1:17.809. Senna wasn't at the test . . .

At Imola in testing Senna did 1:21.244 and in the final moments Schumacher did 1:21.078. Neither driver suggested that these times were definitive, Senna insisting that he hadn't stretched to the fullest, Schumacher accepting the insistence.

The Brazilian Grand Prix at Sao Paulo on the 27th would, as it seemed, be just another opening race to just another season, this one grouped around the expectation of Schumacher versus Senna. In Brazil Senna took pole, but tight.

First Session

	Senna	1:16.386
	Schumacher	1:16.575

Second session

	Senna	1:15.962
	Schumacher	1:16.290

At the green Schumacher got the start wrong. He judged the left-hand side of the circuit, off the racing line, to have less grip. As he lurched forward Senna burst clear, Alesi slotting the Ferrari to mid-track, Hill following Alesi and crowding Schumacher who held him into Turn One, the left-hander. Senna legged it away through the loops and dips and climbs. At the Bico de Pato, a left horseshoe, Schumacher tucked inside Alesi but with such impetus that it drew him full across the track. Alesi tucked inside *him*.

Senna legged it further and further away. On lap 2 Schumacher repeated the move at the Bico de Pato but kept the car tighter and Alesi could only follow. The gap to Senna: 4 seconds. Alesi made a feint or two but Schumacher eased from him and advanced upon Senna. The season tilted then, but only in retrospect. Senna could not escape and a flash reading put the gap at 1.89.

They pitted on lap 21, Senna stationary for 7.8 seconds, Schumacher — further up the pit lane — fractionally quicker. He emerged first and thus into the lead. Senna had to prove everything, catch and dispatch Schumacher, but Schumacher forced a gap of 4.33 and after the second pit-stops 'never really felt under pressure. I could control the gap by pushing a bit hard.' It steadied at 9 seconds and on lap 56 Senna spun out. 'My fault,' he said, 'pushing too hard.' On Senna now the merciless weight of comparison had come.

Schumacher lapped everyone.

It prompts Brundle, who'd joined Marlboro McLaren, to say that 'the guy is awesome. He and Senna were in a class of their own, but in Brazil for instance he got Senna rattled. Schumacher did his job without mistakes, did it brilliantly and won the race. I had a long chat with him there and I couldn't help but be impressed by his maturity and professionalism. He knows what he wants, where he's going and how to go about it.'

At Aida, a new track for a new race — the Pacific Grand Prix — Senna took pole from Schumacher again. Schumacher described how he approached the circuit: 'A bit like you drive a go-kart. It's tiny but very tricky and very technical.' At the green they veered towards each other, flicked away. Into Turn One, a right, Hakkinen bumped Senna and pushed him off, Larini (deputising for Alesi) in the Ferrari ramming him. By the end only Berger stayed on the same lap, and only because Schumacher deliberately circled behind him in the closing laps. 'After the start I wasn't pushed very hard so I could take it very easy with the car, with the tyres, and could run the race home. That's the only intention I had after the start.'

In an interview in *Motoring News* under the headline WHO IS BETTER — SENNA OR SCHUMACHER? Niki Lauda said that the main difference between them is 'their age. A big difference. Presumably God has blessed and gifted both of them with the same amount of talent; then it's only a question of time until Schumacher has the same experience as Senna. And then, thanks to his youth, he will beat — maybe even outdrive — Senna. But Senna will never sleep. Always he will go full throttle.' *Autosport* carried a front page headline SENNA: CAN HE TAKE THE HEAT? with a sub-heading CRUNCH TIME IN SAN MARINO.

Imola was the weekend of mourning, Austrian Roland Ratzenberger's Simtek veering off at 200 mph and hitting a wall on the Saturday. He died in hospital slightly over an hour later. At the green on the Sunday, Lehto stalled and Pedro Lamy (Lotus), unsighted by a car ahead, struck the Benetton hard. Both drivers escaped serious injury but a wheel went into the crowd injuring

No further caption necessary.

Schumacher looking rather more than pensive.

Schumacher was big news by the start of the 1994 season in Brazil.

several spectators. Senna led Schumacher and Berger before the pace car came out and circled while the wreckage was cleared. At the end of lap 5 the pace car peeled off, releasing them.

Schumacher immediately pressured Senna and noticed that through the Tamburello corner Senna's car 'seemed very nervous. I could see that it was bottoming quite a lot and he nearly lost it.' Schumacher continued the pressure and on the next lap 'at the same place Ayrton did lose it. The car's rear skid-plates touched the ground, he got a bit sideways.' Senna braked, and across the brief run-off area cut his speed by some 70 miles an hour, but that still meant he struck the wall at the far side of the run-off area at more than 130 mph. 'It looked a very dangerous impact, but I didn't have the feeling it was anywhere near what happened when Roland crashed,' Schumacher said.

Senna died in hospital.

Eventually the race was re-started and Schumacher won easily enough from Larini. He stood sombre on the podium, hands locked behind his back, his face drawn towards the dignity of bearing grief.

At the next race, Monaco, a British newspaper, *The Mail On Sunday*, quoted Schumacher as saying that if he'd lost the feeling for driving 'I would have stopped. This was the question to myself after Senna: "Michael, if you don't have back the proper feeling, then it is no use. Michael, you have to stop for good." Everything you would do in a car without this feeling of being certain would be dangerous.' Could he have walked away? 'I can't truly know because I have never tried it, but I like to feel I could have been this strong in my mind.'

Weber was quoted as saying, 'He did suffer for a long time. We discussed. Then for hours, for days, he thought. I would not have been surprised if he had decided to walk away. For 20 years I was a race driver and I knew how serious he was. This week [Monaco] you see him more changed than ever before because for the first time in his life he has been put in touch with death.'

Each driver and each team approached Monaco in a personal way, essentially forcing themselves through it, and in Thursday's free practice Wendlinger crashed heavily, was taken to hospital in a coma. 'On Wednesday and Thursday in practice I drove with no feeling, and I was not sure,' Schumacher said. 'Then on Friday it was different. Only then did I feel I could continue my job.'

He had pole from Hakkinen and Berger and the drivers observed a minute's silence for Senna and Ratzenberger before the race. At Ste Devote, Hakkinen and Hill collided, Schumacher moving away from Berger in a decisive, devastating way. He led by nearly 4 seconds at the end of lap 1 and would have only one instant of anxiety, when Mark Blundell's Tyrrell blew and 'I was right behind. I almost hit the barrier.' Schumacher crossed the line 36 seconds in front of Brundle and as he walked to the podium he and Flavio Briatore, Benetton's commercial director, embraced with such emotion that Schumacher was lifted clean off the ground: a curious moment capable of many interpretations, not least that some sort of normality had returned, that a victory could again be celebrated.

Schumacher 40, Berger 10.

Hasty new regulations governing the cars would be in force for the Spanish Grand Prix. Schumacher tested the 'new' Benetton at Jerez and said that it 'slides more and is more sensitive to drive. When you go on the throttle there is more reaction in the corner. It's going to be difficult for the teams which don't have the opportunity to test. We need to do something, but whether this [the change in regulations] is right I'm not sure. The accidents mainly happened because the cars were touching the ground, and to improve things in that area would have been better.'

Main picture *Ayrton Senna at Imola.*

Inset *Imola, the race of starkest tragedy: Senna, Schumacher, Gerhard Berger.*

The Spanish Grand Prix meeting at Barcelona writhed with a turmoil of its own. On the Thursday the drivers gathered and discussed a new chicane, which, using foresight during Monaco, Schumacher had asked to be built before the ultra-fast right-hander at the back of the Catalunya circuit. It hadn't been and some felt that Schumacher should have been at Barcelona early to make sure it had; but, as others pointed out, he'd been testing at Jerez and it's awkward to be at two ends of a country at the same time.

Whatever, the drivers made a clear demand. *Build that chicane or we won't drive.* The drivers won and got themselves twin tyre walls with a little gap in the middle. The gap was widened by 2 metres on the Friday after free practice, a free practice during which only five teams went out. The others were locked in talks with FIA [renamed from FISA] President Max Mosley over the implications of the new regulations.

They all went out in first qualifying, Schumacher quickest from Hakkinen and Hill; on the Saturday Schumacher moved down from the 1:23s to 1:21.908. At the green he led from Hill and increased and increased it. He made his first pit-stop on lap 21, at the same time as Herbert in the Lotus. As they both exited the pit lane, Schumacher first, Herbert following, it seemed entirely ordinary. A new 50 mph limit in the pit lane had been introduced at Monaco and obtained here, too.

They reached the point where they could accelerate and Herbert surged past Schumacher. What could that mean? 'The car was perfect in the beginning and I was able to open up a good lead quite easily,' said Schumacher. 'Then the gearbox wouldn't select gears. All I know is that it was stuck in fifth. When I stopped at the pits I asked if there was anything that could be done but there was nothing.'

'I was completely unaware that he was stuck in fifth,' Herbert says. 'He'd been leading the race, but if he's slower than me I'll pass him. I looked in my mirrors and thought he'd dropped back quite a long way.'

Hakkinen went by, Hill went by, Schumacher third and crippled. He applied his logic to this problem. 'At first it was a bit difficult to take all the corners in fifth, but then I managed to find a good line and keep up reasonable lap times. My experience in Group C helped me in this because I learned a lot of ways of running differently, of changing my driving style, usually to save fuel. I used that same style and it certainly helped me a lot.' The lap times after the stop chart Schumacher doing precisely this. Successively he moved through the 1:31s to the 1:27s in ten laps.

Hakkinen made his stop on lap 31 and Hill on lap 42, giving Schumacher the lead again. Hakkinen's engine let go on lap 48. By then Schumacher had made a second stop, fraught with hazard because he risked stalling as he pulled away. He didn't stall. He looked smooth. 'I had to use a lot of revs and slip the clutch to get going. I gave the engine a lot of punishment but it kept working beautifully.' Hill led to the end, Schumacher slowing to protect his clutch so that the final margin stretched to 24 seconds.

There are telling anecdotes about Jim Clark. Sometimes in a race he'd suddenly slow for a lap or two, then regain his former pace. He'd had a problem, adjusted to it and, in the motor racing phrase, 'drove round it'. For a generation only Senna had been compared to Clark . . .

Ford said that the 'telemetry confirms that following the gearbox failure, the Zetec-R in Schumacher's car was required to pull from a minimum 5,200 rpm on each remaining lap and rev to its maximum 14,500 rpm for long periods on the straights. With his Benetton Ford

Benetton refuel during the Brazilian Grand Prix. It seemed perfectly safe.

stuck in fifth gear, Schumacher's best lap around the 2.95-mile Barcelona circuit was 1:26.17 seconds. There were only three other recorded laps better than that, one of those being Schumacher's own record-setting 1:25.15 seconds — with all gears operative [lap 18].'

'Under the circumstances we couldn't be more pleased with Michael's result,' Steve Parker, Ford's Formula 1 Program Manager, said. 'The fact that he was able to carry on racing despite the loss of all but one gear is eloquent testimony to Michael's superb driving skills, the tractability and strength of Ford's Zetec-R V8 and the brilliance of the Benetton's chassis design. Some journalists were so surprised by this performance that immediately after the race we had to show them the raw telemetry data before they could accept that Michael really had driven the race in fifth gear only.'

Mansell's presence challenged Schumacher — and Hill

In Canada, for the first time since Senna's death Schumacher came under genuine pressure during qualifying. In the first session Alesi hammered in 1:26.277 against 1:26.820.

In the second session *Eurosport* enjoyed one of those moments you can't script. Martin Walters, Chief Engineer of Cosworth engines, went up to their commentary box and chatted to John Watson. Alesi came out and pitched the Ferrari at the circuit, Schumacher also on the circuit. Alesi had the Ferrari twitching and darting and you could feel the effort. 1:26.739. Schumacher looked less nervy although at one point he locked the brakes. 1:26.336. He moved into another fast lap.

Watson: 'A big improvement from Michael Schumacher and he's looking to improve further. Now Martin Walters is sitting here beside us smiling at this performance . . . but Michael again locks up, his fronts this time. Martin, you must be impressed with how he's developed in the three years of your association with him.'

Walters: 'We're very impressed with Michael. I think this year he's more relaxed, we're working much better as a team. We haven't had any distractions from other teams and I think we'll see great things from Michael this year. As John said earlier, I think this is the first race meeting where he's been really pushed, and Michael is now trying as hard as he knows to get pole position.'

Watson: 'As an engineer, how do you explain that ability to convey information between you and Michael Schumacher?'

Walters: 'What you actually have to remember about Michael is that he can drive at this pace and still have enough capacity left in his mind to understand what's going on. At the end of the run he's able to relate to us exactly what the problems are. Are there any hesitations on any of the corners from the engine? Does it pick up cleanly? Does the gearshift pick up nice and clean? For instance, yesterday we had a problem changing from fifth to sixth.'

[At this moment Schumacher completed his lap, 1:26.178, translating to 0.099 quicker than Alesi's Friday time.]

Walters, chuckling: 'I've gone quiet now because he's gone to the front.'

He stayed pole.

Schumacher won the Canadian Grand Prix, which he led from start to finish. After Canada, Schumacher 56 points, Hill 23, Berger 13.

Nigel Mansell returned for the French Grand Prix, generating a vast ground-swell of hype, curiosity and, when he clambered into the Rothmans Williams Renault, respect. Young Scotsman David Coulthard had taken Senna's place in Spain and Canada, but he couldn't hope to challenge Schumacher. Mansell might. His presence — although nobody was saying as much — also represented a challenge to Hill. Meanwhile Jos Verstappen replaced Lehto at Benetton, the team explaining that Lehto hadn't fully recovered from his testing crash in January. That merciless weight.

On the Saturday Mansell and Hill traded fastest laps and for once Schumacher found himself on the second row. He blitzed the start, slicing between the Williamses, Hill clinging, Mansell falling back. 'I couldn't have made a better start,' Schumacher said. 'It was absolutely perfect. I went just as the red light went out. It was a very tough fight at the beginning, but that is what we all enjoy.' This start became a cause of wondering rather than just wonder.

Silverstone, the Thursday, and the pressure hemmed Damon Hill. He faced the press and, head tilted downward, unloaded. 'What do you have to do? That's what I want to know. What do you bloody have to do for people to believe that you're any good? Last weekend I

Schumacher won the Pacific Grand Prix at Aida and Senna had yet to finish a race in the Williams Renault.

beat Nigel Mansell [in France] and the year before that I beat Alain Prost for pole position. I led the race, I came closer to beating Michael Schumacher than anyone's come all year other than Ayrton Senna [in this context Spain hardly counts] and all I get from the papers, all I'm reading about, is my bloody job's in jeopardy.

'I'm second in the World Championship, I've come here to beat Michael Schumacher and try and win this race and try and turn the Championship round. I've never heard such a lot of bollocks in my life as I've heard since last week. [Long pause.] I'm very pissed off. I don't get any credit for being polite and diplomatic so I'm going to ditch that tack because it's not getting me anywhere. [Pause.] I'm fighting a battle here with a car that is clearly not as good as the Schumacher-Benetton combination.

'I need 100 per cent backing from Williams to do the job properly — which I've asked for — and I proved last weekend that I am getting the best out of the equipment. [Pause.] It's taken me ten years to get to this position in Formula 1. I'm not going to relinquish it or give it up to anyone without a serious fight. I promise you I am here to stay. I have proved myself as a top Formula 1 driver and this weekend I will work again to prove that point. That's all I have to say.'

On the Friday Schumacher took provisional pole from Berger, Hill fourth, and after the session Schumacher was leaving the pit area on his scooter. That involved, as it always does, squeezing through the crowd who gather at the gate. All unknowing Schumacher ran over the foot of 10-year-old Ian Foulds from Seaham, County Durham, who stood holding out his autograph book.

Ian was taken to the medical centre to see if any bones had been broken and I set off to Benetton to get some reaction. They expressed astonishment and in turn set off to tell Schumacher, in a technical meeting. He was 'stunned' and left the meeting immediately, jumped on his scooter bearing a tee-shirt for Ian and reached the medical centre only to be told that Ian was fine and had been discharged.

Maybe that set the tone for a peculiar race meeting, Hill taking pole from Schumacher after a rush-rush-rush of a second session where they and Berger traded blows like heavyweights right to the bell. On the warm-up lap before the race Schumacher set off in a cloud of smoke from the tyres, leading Hill — a breach of the rules, which state that cars must remain in grid order. Coulthard couldn't get his engine to fire on the grid so the starting procedure had to be aborted. When they tried a second time, Schumacher took the lead again on the warm-up lap and would subsequently claim that Hill was 'going a bit slow'. The rules are clear: Schumacher ought to have been ordered to start from the back of the grid. That did not happen.

Hill took the lead from Schumacher while the Stewards deliberated, decided on a 5-second penalty and informed Benetton. Crucially the penalty did not include the words 'stop-go'. Briatore said that 'we were told of the penalty but the stop-go wasn't mentioned. Therefore we didn't ask Michael to come into the pits.' Benetton, and Schumacher when they told him over the radio, assumed that the 5 seconds would be added to his total race time and Schumacher faced the problem of overtaking Hill and getting 5 seconds clear of him.

After the early pit stops Schumacher was given the black flag on lap 21. The black flag has always been the ultimate sanction in motor racing and non-negotiable. The driver's number is displayed at the start-finish line and the black flag. The indicated driver must come in. This time negotiations — heated — did take place between Benetton and the Stewards, and for the next two laps Schumacher ignored the black flag. It was then withdrawn.

Schumacher did come in on lap 27 for the stop-go, essentially costing him the race. He was reluctant to discuss it afterwards, and small wonder. The Stewards issued a statement culminating in a decision 'to formally reprimand the competitor Mild Seven Benetton Ford for a lack of a complete understanding of F1 rules and of the need for this to be corrected and for their meticulous application in the future. Michael Schumacher and competitor Mild Seven Benetton Ford were fined US $25,000 for breach of the applicable regulations.'

The turmoil was back already and, more than that, from being the absolute favourite to take the World Championship long before season's end, Schumacher moved into a waking nightmare. Nothing like it had happened since 1976 when another native German speaker, Niki Lauda, and another Briton, James Hunt, contested the Championship amid protests, hearings, appeals, disqualifications and re-instatements. Schumacher's nightmare came at him on a weekly and sometimes daily basis. Leaving Silverstone, Schumacher 72 points, Hill 39. [Please note that in what follows Benetton refer to themselves by their official name, Benetton Formula].

Week 1 (11–17 July): The FIA launched an inquiry into the events of Silverstone, raising the spectre that they might take Schumacher's 6 points from Silverstone away and, following the precedent of Nigel Mansell in Portugal in 1989, ban him from the next race. This was extremely intriguing, because the next race was Hockenheim, already virtually sold out. Would the FIA dare? What would their reputation be if they didn't?

Benetton team manager Joan Villadelprat said, 'We messed up [at Silverstone] but so did the Stewards. The rule says we have to be notified within 15 minutes of the incident.' By now a timetable had been re-created minute by minute, and it showed clearly that Schumacher's original offence — overtaking Hill on the warm-up laps — took place at 2.00, but the Stewards' decision did not reach Benetton until 2.27.

Week 2 (18–24 July): Schumacher was summoned to a meeting of the World Motor Sports Council in Paris on 26 July. The following were also summoned: Rubens Barrichello and Mika Hakkinen (who'd crashed on the last lap at Silverstone), Damon Hill (who'd allegedly stopped on his slowing-down lap to gather a Union Jack, stopping now illegal), representatives of Benetton and Pierre Aumonier, clerk of the course.

*Senna's memory hung heavy over Monaco. Schumacher's victory was the
first step in bringing a semblance of normality back.*

Schumacher was quoted as saying, 'It is all a lot of hot air and I don't think it is right to interfere with the Championship like this. All the theatre is rather stupid.' He tested at Silverstone for three days — the Tuesday, Wednesday and Thursday — and did a best time of 1:27.28 against Hill's 1:26.96. The importance of this test cannot be overstated. All teams had to run stepped flat-bottom cars at Hockenheim, meaning a plank of wood under the car to reduce down-force. It wasn't quite as primitive as that, but never mind.

'Overall, after this test, I feel very confident,' Schumacher said. 'The car is certainly more difficult to drive but it has been a productive session. You have to lift considerably more now and it has been important to get a good ride in the car.'

Week 3 (25–31 July): Schumacher, wearing a multi-coloured sports jacket (nice not garish) cut a path through the media and went into the FIA headquarters, Place de la Concorde, Paris, on the Tuesday. After the hearing he lost his 6 points from Silverstone and was given a two-race ban. He faced a dilemma. If he accepted the ban he missed Hockenheim. If he lodged an appeal — and he had seven days to do that — he could drive at Hockenheim but risk having the ban increased if the appeal failed. The talk was of precedents again.

Monaco. Schumacher, Briatore and smiles of relief that nothing had happened except a motor race and a victory.

Jordan's Eddie Irvine had been given a one-race ban after crashing in the Brazilian Grand Prix, subsequently raised to three when his appeal failed. Leaving the Place de la Concorde, Schumacher 66 points, Hill 39.

Benetton were fined $500,000 for their failure to obey the Stewards' orders at Silverstone and a further $100,000 for being tardy in producing 'source codes' for their electronic systems, which the FIA had been demanding since the San Marino Grand Prix. This is a dark part of the nightmare. Benetton were found to have a system that *could* be in breach of the regulations. In essence, as we have seen, the regulations prevented computers from controlling the cars; but the FIA found no evidence that the system had been used. (This did not prevent fevered speculation on Schumacher's astonishing start in the French Grand Prix, where, remember, he'd blitzed it.)

Benetton reacted firmly. 'Both Michael Schumacher and the Benetton Formula team feel that the penalties inflicted on them were very severe. Together both parties have agreed to appeal in front of the International Court of Appeal of the FIA through the respective National Sporting Authorities, and therefore Michael Schumacher will take part in the upcoming 1994 German Grand Prix. This decision has been reached following the concern from both Michael Schumacher and the Benetton Formula team that Michael's absence from his home Grand Prix would unfairly penalise and disappoint all the German fans who have long awaited this event. Michael Schumacher and the Benetton Formula hope that this appeal will result in a decreased penalty. Their priority now is to prepare for a winning performance this weekend.'

So to Hockenheim, where, commenting on what happened in Paris, Schumacher said that 'obviously they didn't believe me that I didn't see the black flag. I'm really sorry that I didn't see the black flag, that I haven't taken care about the black flag, but if you don't see it you don't come in, you do your race. You continue.'

On the Friday an immense crowd watched Schumacher qualify third behind Hill and, gloriously, Berger in the Ferrari. In the nightmare it could not be so simple. During the morning untimed session, Verstappen went off and in their zeal the marshals doused the car with so much extinguishant that it needed new wiring, engine and gearbox. The car could not be readied for first qualifying so Schumacher had a run, then passed it to Verstappen and 'at the second chicane I suddenly spun on to the gravel. I feel really sorry having ruined Michael's qualifying.'

On the Saturday Schumacher went only fourth fastest, Berger and Alesi filling the front row. It put Schumacher on the second row with Hill. 'I don't really care about my grid position here. What I do care about is the job we've done, and that's been superb. It's been a hundred per cent effort by everyone in the team and we have improved the car a lot.' He talked of perhaps a podium finish.

Week 4 (1–7 August): Race day at Hockenheim and a wild start to the race. Berger got away fast, and so did Alesi, but mayhem towards the back of the grid. Cars bumped and spun: De Cesaris in the Sauber, Zanardi in the Lotus, Alboreto and Martini in the Minardis. Hakkinen (McLaren) went deep to the inside, running along the pit lane wall looking for an advantage. Approaching the first, curving-right, corner Hakkinen moved over on Coulthard and tapped him. That pitched the McLaren full across the track and across the rest of the grid. It skimmed directly in front of Blundell's Tyrrell and, Blundell already on the brakes, Barrichello could do nothing but perform a battering-ram on the Tyrrell. By now cars were moving in bewildering directions and the real perspective is that — Alesi out with electrics — 11 cars had gone after a single lap. And Hill had been tapped by Katayama's Tyrrell on that first lap — he'd lose more than 3 minutes in the pits.

Schumacher hustled Berger, attacked, and Berger resisted. 'I tried very hard to overtake. I put the Ferrari under a lot of pressure and I felt sure I could have taken the lead eventually.' Schumacher pitted for tyres and fuel after 12 laps, resumed in second place. Verstappen followed into the pits three laps later. The car stopped but the fuel nozzle wouldn't go into the entrance to the fuel tank properly. Fuel belched out, became spray like torrential rain and the instant it touched the hot, hot, hot engine the car seemed to explode. Verstappen and the crew still changing the wheels were engulfed in a molten yellow wall of fire that rose 10 feet into the air with a mush-room cloud of black smoke above it.

Some images you'll never forget.

That Verstappen survived with comparatively minor burns and only one of the crew was burned is frankly unbelievable. Like Berger's crash and fire at Imola in 1989, the more times you replay it on video the more you are sure — absolutely sure — the driver cannot survive.

The race went on and after 20 laps Schumacher 'suddenly had a problem. I've no idea what it was but the engine seemed to lose power. I'm very, very disappointed for the supporters who gave me such great support during the weekend.' Hill finished second, so that leaving tree-lined, concrete-clad Hockenheim, Schumacher 66 points, Hill 39.

The images weren't of any of that but of Verstappen.

'The mechanics are now scared, and when you are scared you make mistakes'

On the Tuesday a team statement said that 'Benetton Formula are carrying out a thorough investigation into the events leading to the fire and until this investigation is complete we will not be making any further comment. However, Benetton Formula would like to commend the actions of their staff in dealing with the fire in such a professional manner. In common with other teams in Formula 1, Benetton Formula staff had been trained in fire-fighting techniques, the benefit of which was clearly demonstrated. A small number of staff received superficial injuries in the fire and we wish them a very speedy recovery. Benetton Formula are aware that certain team members made comments following the incident and expressed their disapproval with regards to refuelling. We would like to point out that the comments made naturally came from the emotions provoked by the incident.'

That week Briatore said, 'When I went back to the factory and saw the faces of the mechanics who had been burned I said, "Jesus, we have to stop this." We could even do it immediately and if necessary have shorter races for the people who don't have enough fuel capacity. I saw that the mechanics are now scared, and when you are scared you make mistakes more easily.'

Intertechnique, who made the refuelling equipment that all Formula 1 teams used, were delegated by the FIA to examine that of Benetton on the Wednesday at Witney, Oxfordshire, the team's base. After the fireball, a time-bomb.

The unbelievable drive in Spain. Schumacher, stuck in fifth gear, still finished second.

Week 5 (8–14 August): The FIA ignited it on the Wednesday. 'The fuel spillage was caused by the fuel valve failing to close properly. The valve was slow to close due to the presence of a foreign body. The foreign body is believed to have reached the valve because a filter designed to eliminate the risk had been deliberately removed.' One estimate — not the FIA's — estimated that, by removing the filter, fuel would have flowed in at 12.5 per cent faster, saving perhaps a second during the pit-stop — and Formula 1 teams are always looking to save a second. Formula 1 teams *think* in terms of seconds.

The FIA statement implied, in stark terms, that Benetton had deliberately compromised safety, with all that that involved, to steal an advantage. Would the FIA banish Benetton from Formula 1? Would that be the end of Schumacher's Championship? Benetton struck back immediately with an explosion of their own. They said this:

Following the press release issued today by the FIA regarding the fire involving Car no 6 during a Pit Stop at the German Grand Prix, Benetton Formula Ltd would like to make the following statement:

Benetton Formula's concern for an investigation into the events surrounding the incident prompted us to contract an independent company specialising in accident investigation to carry out a study of the accident and to give an opinion on the method of refuelling.

This company is a specialist in the field of accident investigation and assessment of engineering failures and accidents. They particularly specialise in the aerospace field.

The company has conducted investigations into over 300 serious accidents worldwide, in addition to numerous less serious cases. Their work has included involvement in most major accidents since 1972 to public transport aircraft and helicopters in the UK, and surrounding waters, as well as overseas incidents where aircraft of UK registration or manufacture have been involved.

The company has also frequently served as technical investigator for military boards of inquiry into serious and complex military aircraft accidents.

Part of their report states:

Consideration was given to the effect of the absence of the filter previously positioned at the point where the inner hose joins the nozzle unit (it is understood

The Canadian victory acclaimed.

that this was removed for the Hockenheim Race after a lengthy period during which no debris was collected in any of the Benetton team's filters).

Any debris would, under normal circumstances, travel through the connection into the car tank. No evidence was seen, during the examination of scouring or of other effects, which could have resulted from debris fouling any of the moving parts. A study of the layout of the fuel path and of the evidence surrounding the incident did not suggest any way in which any feasible debris contamination from the fuel flow could have caused the failure of the nozzle to engage correctly.'

Given our concern over refuelling safety, we had hoped to be able to discuss this report with FIA and undertake the necessary actions to reduce the risks involved in refuelling. A written request has now been placed with the FIA urgently requesting such a meeting.

A copy of this report was immediately lodged with our legal advisers, Marriott Harrison of London, upon receipt of the FIA's press release.

The filter mentioned was introduced part way through the year in response to problems teams were having with debris entering the valve and car. Benetton was able to eliminate this problem.

The Benetton fuel rigs prior to Hockenheim had been thoroughly stripped and cleaned and there was no risk of debris entering the valve assembly. Benetton also pre-filter their fuel twice before it is placed in the fuel rig.

Benetton Formula concluded the filter was unnecessary and it was removed with the full knowledge and permission of the FIA Formula 1 Technical delegate, Mr Charlie Whiting. This permission was given on the afternoon of Thursday 28 July to Mrs Joan Villadelprat in the presence of Mr Ross Brawn [Technical Director].

The consequence of attributing, in Benetton Formula's view incorrectly, the cause of this fire to the lack of a filter means that such an incident could happen again, possibly with far more serious consequences.'

The World Motor Sport Council summoned Benetton to the Place de la Concorde on 19 October. Only two races would remain after that, Japan and Australia. During Week 5 the season and the Championship had disintegrated into more or less anything you wanted it to be in your imagination; and if you enjoyed mental arithmetic — or even riddles — you could play endlessly. Schumacher was appealing against Silverstone, which might cost him more than missing two races; Benetton might be retrospectively kicked out of the Championship *when Schumacher had already won it*. Schumacher might win his appeal. Benetton might defend themselves well . . .

On the Friday Schumacher took provisional pole from Hill; and confirmed it on the Saturday. The boy could take pressure, could isolate every external influence and just drive. You can't if you can't, if you see what I mean. Some say the adrenalin and urgency of the act of driving at these speeds inevitably precludes every external influence. Me? I'm not so sure. The most *aware* human beings you're ever likely to meet are Formula 1 drivers, and they prosper by isolating one train of thought from another train of thought; and they learn the mechanisms for doing it.

Week 6 (15–21 August): Hill made the better start to the Hungarian Grand Prix and, on the inside, found himself better positioned for Turn One. Schumacher drove clean round the outside and squeezed Hill so hard that he was half into a little tarmac run-off area. Nothing serious. 'I had a good start but then I had too much wheel-

Inevitably, Schumacher had been the focus of the Hockenheim weekend.

The thousands willed Schumacher on but he didn't finish the German Grand Prix.

spin and Damon was able to pull alongside going into the first corner. In fact, he was slightly ahead but I knew that if I stayed alongside I would be OK through the next corner and that's how it worked out. I then had some pressure because I did not know what the Williams pit-stop tactics would be. I was stopping three times and that meant I had to push hard to make sure I kept my advantage. Once I made my final stop I was able to ease off a bit. Winning this race has taken away much of the pressure on us.'

Only the juggle of pit-stops took the lead from Schumacher (from laps 17 to 25), and thereafter he ran for home smooth and isolated as you like, beating Hill by some 20 seconds, Verstappen third. Schumacher no doubt revealed a bit and concealed a bit of his feelings when he said that 'after all the recent happenings, this was a truly great result for the team. Everybody has been a little bit nervous all weekend but now we can relax and I was very happy for Jos to finish on the rostrum for the first time, which made it a very special day for everybody in the team.'

'Schumacher was considering leaving Benetton over the fuel filter affair'

Well, yes, and not a protest in sight. What was this, just a motor race? We'd forgotten what they were. Leaving stately, earthy Budapest and its infuriating motor racing circuit in the bleached hillocks outside it, Schumacher 76 points, Hill 45.

Schumacher tested at Silverstone on the Wednesday, managing 20 laps when it wasn't raining. On the Thursday he stayed in the car a lot longer and towards the end got down to 1:27.16 against the next best, Hill, on 1:27.68.

Week 7 (22–28 August): Maurice Hamilton, writing in the London *Observer*, claimed that Schumacher was considering leaving Benetton over the fuel filter affair and quoted him as saying that 'for me, honesty is the most important thing'. Hamilton is the most meticulous of motor racing writers and completely uninterested in sensationalism, so what he does write carries both authenticity and authority. Benetton wouldn't say a word about what Hamilton said Schumacher was saying.

On the Tuesday Benetton announced that they had signed a three-year contract with Renault for use of their engines, thanking Ford for 'an invaluable and dynamic relationship'. Williams would be keeping Renault engines too — interesting for 1995.

On the Friday Barrichello in the Sasol Jordan took provisional pole by waiting until the end of a wet-drying session and risking slicks. Schumacher was next, then Hill. Schumacher had risked slicks himself but spun on his last lap. He thought it would have been a pole lap if he hadn't. 'I made a mistake and it cost me. I hadn't adjusted the brake balance properly so I locked the rear brakes.' On the Saturday, wet again, no change to the top of the grid: Barrichello had become, at 22, the youngest driver ever to take pole, and did a war-dance to celebrate the instant the session ended — but not an instant before it ended, just in case.

Week 8 (29 August–4 September): A dry race at Spa, Barrichello keeping his nerve at the green light, Schumacher behind and pitching the car right then left searching for an opening. Barrichello held Schumacher to Les Combes, the right-left-right out in the country. Schumacher powered round the outside of him. Order: Schumacher, Barrichello, Alesi, Hill. It became a typical Schumacher race, power and poise applied to maximum effect and only one moment of danger when, on lap 19, he spun and rode the kerbing, but gathered it up quickly and cleanly enough. He led the first lap by 2.5 seconds, forced that up to 4.2 after the second lap and beat Hill by 13.662 seconds. 'My car was really sensitive on the throttle this time and it was difficult, but I think in the end it was difficult for everyone. Certainly we managed somehow to have a car which from the beginning was even more competitive.' Leaving the tree-lined Ardennes, Schumacher 86, Hill 51.

The Stewards checked the Benetton and whispering began that all wasn't well. At 8.20 in the evening the Stewards announced that the plank under the Benetton had not conformed to the regulations and Benetton's points were being taken from them. The plank had to be 10 mm deep with an allowance of 10 per cent wear during a race, meaning that it must measure a minimum 9 mm afterwards. The Stewards claimed that in some places it measured only 7.4 mm. In defence, Ross Brawn, the team's Technical Director, argued that it might have been Schumacher's spin that had ground down the plank.

Benetton lodged an immediate appeal. Leaving a by now darkened and desolate Ardennes, Schumacher 76, Hill 55.

On the Tuesday Schumacher tramped the familiar route across the Place de la Concorde (wearing a different jacket this time) and made his appeal against the two-race ban over the Silverstone black flag. It was rejected. Evidently when Schumacher saw his number — 5 — hoisted he assumed that it meant a 5-second penalty. 'We thought we had good arguments, but it turned out they were not good enough.' In the media scrum when he emerged, someone asked if he'd leave Formula 1. 'I need a few days to think about a lot of things. When I make a decision, or need to make a decision, I will let you know, but at the moment nothing has changed for me.'

In another sense, of course, a great deal had changed for him. Five races remained, and if Hill won the two that Schumacher must now miss — Italy and Portugal — that cut the difference to a single point between them; with the Benetton explanation over the Hockenheim fire and the Spa plank appeal still looming, ghosts in the nightmare. Benetton might be out of it altogether or Schumacher might conjure 10 points back from the darkness — which presumably would relegate Hill to second again at Spa, costing Hill 4 points. Yes, yes, I know that at most sporting events you don't need to wait weeks for the result, but . . .

The FIA had abandoned the absurdity of waiting until 19 October to adjudicate on the fire, and instead of hearing the plank appeal on Monday 5 September and the fire explanation at dear old Place de la Concorde on Wednesday 7 September, they'd do the two for the price of one on the Wednesday in Paris. At least nobody at Benetton would need a street map to find it.

Week 9 (5–11 September): The German newspaper *Welt-am-Sonntag* (*World on Sunday*) quoted Schumacher as saying that 'if it is established that the team have been doing things behind my back which are forbidden by the rules, I would not accept that. By that I mean that I could move to another team.'

On the Monday Benetton announced that Lehto would join Verstappen for the Italian Grand Prix at Monza, and presumably for Portugal, too.

Schumacher didn't go to Paris on the Wednesday, where the World Motorsport Council decreed that the Spa appeal had been rejected,

The Schumacher-Hill struggle had its lighter moments. Here they are on the podium in Hungary.

but there was insufficient evidence to take further action against the team over the fire.

Benetton said: 'The Mild Seven Benetton Ford Formula 1 Team is very pleased with the result of today's hearing in Paris, which has completely cleared its good name from any allegations of cheating. Whilst the team may not have been able to satisfy the World Council as to the precise cause of the wear to the skid board, it was delighted that the FIA stated in clear terms that there was no question of the team cheating.

'The team has also been completely cleared of the charge of removing the fuel filter illegally. This should put an end to unfounded and wild speculations in the press that the removal of the filter caused the fire at Hockenheim. Before the hearing the FIA conceded that it was not alleging that the removal of the filter had caused the fire. In giving the World Council's decision, the President (Max Mosley) stated that its unanimous view was that the filter was removed in complete good faith and that it would be inappropriate to impose any penalty whatsoever.'

Briatore said that 'now the team's good name has been upheld we can concentrate on doing what we do best, winning races. We look forward to Michael Schumacher's return at the Jerez Grand Prix.'

A single task faced Verstappen and Lehto, to beat Damon Hill around Monza's parkland and Estoril's slopes, and protect Schumacher's Championship lead until he returned to protect it himself from Jerez to the climax, wherever and whatever that would be. The nightmare could not be over yet because — you know how it is in nightmares — Schumacher was completely helpless until Jerez.

Hill won Monza and judged 'this victory was well deserved by the team', while Schumacher watched from a restaurant in Monte Carlo. During the following week Williams confirmed that Hill would be staying with them for 1995. That offered peace of mind because the presence of Mansell, returned from IndyCar racing in America, loomed. If Williams had signed Mansell instead — and with young Scotsman David Coulthard progressing superbly in the Williams before Mansell's return — it might have cost Hill the drive.

Hill won Portugal, a race Schumacher watched on television in Germany. 'It's a magic result,' Hill said, 'and I have a great sense of relief because I know people have been considering these last two races, when Michael has been away, as a foregone conclusion.' Schumacher 76, Hill 75, the point made, if you see what I mean.

During the week after that, the suspension served, Schumacher and Benetton tested at Estoril, and so did Hill and Williams. Reportedly Schumacher and Hill shared the same hotel but sat at opposite ends of the dining room during meals. Schumacher did a best time of 1 minute 18.75 seconds, Hill next with 1 minute 19.33. 'I hope that gives Damon some sleepless nights,' Schumacher said. 'I had been looking forward to driving the car again for so long [four weeks, a lifetime in Formula 1] and it was great to be back.' Brawn added that 'Michael revelled in being back . . .'

Incidentally, apart from watching Hill win his two 'missing' races on television, Schumacher had been turning the negative into the positive during his enforced absence. He went to Switzerland and worked, worked, worked on his physical condition, building his strength. 'I did six to eight hours every day at 2,000 metres and it paid off. I felt really great.'

Immediately before Jerez Schumacher launched an astonishing and untypical personal tirade against Hill, which was the equivalent of the world going wild in a quite different way. 'I don't think we would have been in this situation [in the Championship] if Ayrton Senna had been in the car. Ayrton would have been driving circles around me. That shows what I think about Damon as a driver. He has been thrown into the Number One driver position but he never really was a Number One driver. With David Coulthard driving quicker than him after three races, it proves he is not a Number One driver. So the respect is certainly not as much as I have for other drivers.

'You always start to know when you are in trouble and he has not been very helpful when I was in big trouble. Every time we proved we

Belgium and the deceptive victory. Schumacher, disqualified, found himself walking the plank. Mind you, he brought plenty of support.

On his way to The Win That Never Was.

did not cheat they found a way to turn it around and say, "Yes, but there was something else." A lot of people were unhappy with what happened to us, only one or two thought it was right, and one person in particular. I did respect him more in the past because I thought he was a nice guy and a fair guy. A lot of drivers have said fair things, but Damon was the opposite. I don't expect him to stick up for me and say what is happening is wrong, but I don't expect someone to make it even worse. He would have been better to say nothing at all.

'As soon as I saw what he had said, I thought, "OK, now I know how to handle it." This has made me more determined to win the Championship. I always get stronger when I am in trouble. I am certainly more determined because there is one point between us and if I win the title I will have done it in 12 races, not 16. If I don't win the Championship, I think everyone will know why' — the 'missing' races, plus disqualification at Silverstone, plus Benetton's disqualification at the Belgian Grand Prix.

Hill guarded his dignity. 'I'd rather not drag the Championship down by trying to diminish the reputation of the opposition. I think that's sad. Formula 1 has been in that situation for too long, with the two protagonists seemingly hating each other's guts. I think that's bad for Formula 1 and bad for sport, especially in a season when we've lost such a great champion in Ayrton.'

The European Grand Prix turned on pit-stop strategy. Hill led from Schumacher, and Hill intended to make only two stops, Schumacher three. If you compute a pit-stop as 20 seconds (slowing down, stationary for fuel and tyres, emerging slowly) Schumacher seemed very vulnerable. The Benetton action plan: give Schumacher a light fuel load from the start to burst off into the distance, then make the subsequent stops at his leisure (if you can put it like that). Instead Schumacher was captive behind Hill and pitted earlier than foreseen, partly because his tyre pressures weren't quite right and this affected the Benetton's handling.

Williams responded by bringing Hill in three laps later, and two problems arose simultaneously. Hill's stop was slower than Schumacher's, giving Schumacher the lead, and there was a fault with the gauge on the Williams re-fuelling equipment. It delivered 13 litres more than it said it had, which translated to six laps's worth. Those six laps would have been run at high speed, the fuel load lightening moment by moment,

Stunning Schumacher, back after suspension, wins the European Grand Prix at Jerez. (ICN UK Bureau)

Schumacher and Hill exchanged hard words during the Championship's tense final stages and then made it up. (ICN UK Bureau)

but the team couldn't know those 13 litres were in there. They did know something was wrong. Schumacher pitted again on lap 33 of the 69, Hill two laps later. The Williams crew (using Mansell's rig on Hill's car to circumvent whatever the problem was, but itself creating a logistical problem) gave Hill 105 litres to finish the race, but of course the unknown 13 litres were still in there, too. Hill had to haul this load to the end and quite possibly it cost him a second a lap.

Schumacher made his third stop at his leisure and won by some 25 seconds. 'This result is exactly what I wanted after having to miss the two races. I knew I could pick up time when I realised Damon was making two stops to my three and it worked brilliantly.' Schumacher 86, Hill 81.

'I was on the radio every lap to keep informed on Michael's progress'

They went to Suzuka, Herbert replacing Verstappen. The merciless weight of comparison: across ten races Verstappen had scored no more than 10 points. At Suzuka Hill broke the Championship open by mastering insidious, invisible, stalking pressure knowing that *if* he failed to master it, *if* he finished second to Schumacher, he faced a mathematical morass at Adelaide.

Schumacher had pole, Hill alongside on the front row, but heavy rain, almost a storm, drenched and drowned the circuit. Schumacher led, Hill in behind, but Herbert, third, aquaplaned off on lap 4. He was not alone — he was the fifth retirement. The pace car came out and those who remained followed it for seven laps before it peeled off. They raced again but by lap 14 another six cars had gone, stopping the whole thing. This created that nervous mechanism of mental arithmetic, the aggregate. Schumacher's lead of 6.8 seconds from Part One would be carried forward as a weapon into the 36 laps of Part Two after the re-start of the race.

Benetton made a crucial error because Schumacher pitted for fuel twice, Hill only once, so that after Schumacher's second stop, on lap 40 of 50, Hill led on the aggregate by 15 seconds. Schumacher, sensing that he could virtually settle the Championship now, attacked and cut this gap by a couple of seconds a lap. Ghostly, it was, two cars widely separated on the track but one catching the other *on time*. Physically they would never glimpse each other, mentally they both knew the shark-nosed Benetton was taking big, big bites. Not quite a feeding frenzy, but close. Schumacher chewed that gap from 10.1 seconds through 8.3, 7.0, 5.2, 4.2 to the denouement: as they fled into the final lap Hill led on the aggregate by 2.4. Hill had handled it as to the manner born. 'I was on the radio every lap to keep myself informed of Michael's progress.' Hill held the Williams steady, the conditions still full of lurking dangers, and made no mistake; and he had a clear road on that last lap. Schumacher faced two back-markers. They didn't slow him but equally their presence and the dispatching of them prevented him from going for the kill. Hill had it by 3.365. He was naturally unaware of that as he toured on the slowing-down lap. 'There were about four people trying to get on the radio to tell me that I was P1 [Position, First], but there was so much interference that all I could hear was P-blah-blah. I had to tell everyone to calm down, shut up and tell me where I'd finished!' And they did, and they did.

The gap between them stood at the single point, but it magnified itself. If Schumacher finished anywhere in front of Hill at Adelaide he had the Championship. Hill had to think in terms of gaining 2 points over Schumacher, which meant winning or finishing second and holding Schumacher to third. The descending scale of points for the top six finishers in any race — 10, 6, 4, 3, 2, 1 — held Hill rigidly, and a tie on points was useless to Hill because Schumacher still had it on the most-wins tie-break, another rigidity. Approaching Adelaide, only a week after Suzuka, that stood untouchably 8–6 to Schumacher.

Hill arrived in Australia on the Tuesday and spent two days as a guest of former World 500 cc motor bike Champion Barry Sheene, the cockney now living on the Gold Coast in the north. Hill relaxed, swam, prepared himself and then, when he arrived at Adelaide, gave an amazing Press Conference, forcibly complaining that he was under-paid, that he sometimes felt the team wasn't fully behind him.

Patrick Head, the forthright Williams Engineering Director, continued the quiver. 'He's having a whine and a whinge and as far as I am concerned the sooner the first practice starts, the better. Looking at the situation dispassionately, we have to overcome the odds to win. If I were a betting man and I had 100,000 dollars I would be putting it on Schumacher; but that is not meant to undermine Damon.' Whether it undermined Damon or not, it gathered a shriek of headlines.

In first qualifying, to complicate everything, Mansell took provisional pole.

Mansell	1:16.179
Schumacher	1:16.197
Hill	1:16.830

Two minutes from the end of the session, and going beyond the limit, Schumacher spun heavily into the barrier as he tried one last time to beat Mansell. Was the pressure reaching Schumacher? A filthy wet second session left these times undisturbed and now the pressure shifted, also, on to Mansell. He had to help Hill but, if they ran in grid order in the race, how could he orchestrate that? Someone suggested that he might — I am being diplomatic — indulge in the unethical, and Mansell controlled his anger with momentary difficulty. 'That is a disgusting question. I'm above that.' Meanwhile Schumacher murmured, 'No, I'm not bothered about Nigel being in front of me.'

In the build-up to each Grand Prix, a publicity company called Proaction produces a lap of the forthcoming circuit. Before Adelaide they asked Hakkinen for his.

I think they have changed the first corner so I am not too sure about that part of the circuit, but if we look at a lap of the track it goes like this. Ignoring the first corner, you then head for the first tight 90-degree right-hander, which used to be very bumpy under braking. Hit the kerb on the left-hand side and you lose control immediately. You can brake very late but it is tricky. The left-hander is again very bumpy and it is easy to lose the back end. It is particularly difficult as there is very little grip at the entry to the turn . . .

Adelaide, of course, is a street circuit, and although, mercifully, no rain threatened — which would have made overtaking all but impossible — the start might be the crucible, the matrix of the complete race. In the dry, overtaking is very, very difficult. At the green light Mansell's Williams wobbled under the whaaack of acceleration and that was enough to allow Schumacher to draw level. Mansell moved to mid-track but by then Schumacher was ahead, the three cars arranged in a stagger: Schumacher, Mansell, Hill. Leading, Schumacher twisted smooth and safe through the corkscrew of the chicane at the end of the start-finish straight, Hill nipping inside Mansell. They travelled down Wakefield Road to the 90-degree right, travelled to the bumpy left-hander and Mansell went off onto a wedge of grass so verdant it might have been a lawn, scrambled back — but fifth. It left Hill alone and friendless to pursue Schumacher. He had been there before, most of the season.

On lap 2 Hill set fastest lap and started to draw up. The gap crossing the line: 3/10ths, and if you blinked you missed it. Schumacher forced it up to just under 2 seconds and held it there, sometimes a bit more, sometimes a bit less; but that wasn't the story of the race because Hill hadn't cracked. He applied a tourniquet of pressure on Schumacher lap on lap, keeping the Williams just there, always there, and Schumacher couldn't shed him.

They pitted together, emerged together, resumed in tandem. Hill sensed that Schumacher was 'feeling the pressure'. Hill lost nothing as they moved through the back-markers, matching Schumacher move for move, nerve against nerve, in that particularly uncertain art. Fleetingly Hill thrust the Williams directly behind the Benetton but never close enough to risk an outright challenge. They travelled down

Schumacher leads the soaking Japanese Grand Prix from Hill, but the pit stop strategy went wrong. (ICN UK Bureau)

Adelaide, 1994: the picture that went instantly around the world. Glimpsed through the perimeter wire, Schumacher is airborne after colliding with Damon Hill. (AP/Mark Brock)

Wakefield Road and through the 90-degree right, followed almost immediately by the left.

The shark-nosed Benetton should have taken that left smooth and safe, just the way Schumacher had made it do 35 times before. Hill was some distance behind, but anyway it wasn't an overtaking place. A moment later and without any warning everything changed with stark, savage speed. The Benetton turned in, but, as Schumacher would say, 'I got caught on a bump and the car went sideways.' It slewed out of control, scrabbled over multi-coloured kerbing, skittered across the wedge of grass and slapped into a concrete wall; it twitched on impact and bounded back, digging whispers of dust as it went.

The Benetton returned to the track diagonally and at that instant Hill *had* taken the left smooth and safe and was upon it. He had not seen Schumacher hit the wall, only Schumacher's returning. He did not have any chance to gauge the extent of the damage to the Benetton. Hill's impetus was so great that he had to make the Williams veer or strike the rear of the Benetton. The symmetry: both cars within touching distance and *both* diagonal. The mouth of the next corner, a hard right, sucked. In mid-track Schumacher regained control, straightening the Benetton but only when he was far over to the *left*. Hill, hypersensitive, had already straightened the Williams. A millisecond later that hypersensitivity told Hill that a broad gap had opened to the *right*, perfect for the beckoning corner. A flash reading in Hill's mind. *I have to go now.* If only he'd seen Schumacher strike the wall and been able to gauge, 'I wouldn't have gone . . .'

He angled the Williams towards the gap and straightened it there, feeling towards the corner. Schumacher began to turn in himself, but that could only mean turning full across Hill and, under the laws of geometry, into him. The impact forced Hill over curved kerbing at virtually the apex of the corner, Schumacher airborne. The Benetton ran grotesquely, balanced only on the rim of its front and rear left wheels, its underbelly panoramically presented to Hill; but the Benetton was running from Hill and off the circuit again. It righted itself, bounced on all four wheels, skittered over a tight run-off area and head-butted the tyre wall. 'I went to turn into the corner and suddenly I saw Damon next to me and we just hit each other. I drove over his front wheel and I went up in the air. I was afraid because I thought I was going to roll over, but the car came back.' He'd add that after contact with the concrete wall his steering wasn't working properly.

Hill continued round the corner, continued along the short straight and disappeared round the bend at the end of it. 'This was the worst moment,' Schumacher said, 'not being able to continue and yet seeing my rival still driving.' As Schumacher unbuckled his seat belts, levered himself from the Benetton and trotted off tugging at his gloves, Hill need finish only fifth.

On foot, Schumacher reached another concrete wall and clambered over through a gap between it and the protective mesh fence above it. He could not know that Hill was limping back on the long journey to the pits, slowing. Schumacher removed his helmet and stood unconsciously chewing his lip. Hill reached the pits with a wheel locked. Worse, a wishbone on the front suspension had bent. He sat in the cockpit and the clock flickered, 7 seconds stationary, 8, 9, 10, 11, 12.

At 12 he shook his head. He lifted the visor on his helmet and his eyes seemed enlarged, incredulous, saddened, resigned, perhaps embittered. The clock no longer held meaning. Mechanics, urgent uniformed figures flitting to and fro, gathered at the wishbone and felt it, probed it. A gloved hand, gentle as a caress, touched the wishbone where it had bent like a crease. Another gloved hand gripped it there, moved it up and down testing its strength — or its weakness.

Hill sat motionless.

Schumacher stood behind the concrete wall so far away, the lip he had been chewing pursed now. He waited for Hill to come round again, waited to watch his Championship pass by.

They stopped working on Hill's car. Still he sat motionless.

Schumacher's tongue scoured his lip, moistening it because the tension had dried it so much. He watched a Williams come quickly, quickly, quickly towards him, but it had a red number 2 on its snout. That was Mansell, not Hill. Schumacher heard on the loudspeakers that Hill 'had a problem but I wasn't sure what kind of problem'. He watched Mansell go by a second time, a third, no sign of Hill at all. 'Then I thought, *that's it*.'

Hill waited in the pits in the car that could not be mended in time. He sat hoping something could be done, the only chance left that he had. Further up the pit lane the Benetton team watched. Hill got out and walked away by himself. The Benetton mechanics unleashed themselves from their rigidity, danced up and down, embraced, waved to the crowd.

Deep into the Williams pit Hill took his helmet off and the loudspeakers were proclaiming he was out. Schumacher wandered off shaking his head in wonder and initial realisation while a forest of spectators' hands reached out to him. He slapped a few affectionately, shook a couple. Schumacher wandered back to where he had been standing, his whole face lost in a grin and still the hands reached out to touch him. He leant against the protective wire mesh, his fist drawn like a shield to his forehead in order that the wire didn't cut it. In the Williams pit Hill raised his fist and levered his arm downwards in a compressed gesturing of despair and mouthed something — not an obscenity, which he didn't need, but a profound protest against fate, which plays such melodies on human ambition.

A Championship lost and won, here and gone.

Adelaide, 1994 World Champion. (Steve Etherington, Empics)

Hill faced the microphones and said, 'I've a bit of an empty feeling but I gave him a good run for his money. He was certainly feeling the pressure because he ended up falling off the road. I saw the opportunity and I thought *I've got to go here.* I didn't make it. That's motor racing. I am not going to be drawn on the interpretation of what happened. I am very disappointed for my family as much as myself. I want to say that everyone in the Rothmans Williams Renault team deserves a medal this year. They have been through a hell of a tough time and here we were fighting for the Championship and looking very strong and competitive.' He did not compromise on his natural dignity, which is what a big man does when the melodies have taunted; didn't cast deep into the well of perceived injustice.

'I was still in front of Damon, I drove over his front wheel, it was still my corner'

Mansell won the Australian Grand Prix from Berger and Brundle although, as the new Champion, Schumacher joined them to face the world's Press. After some typical Berger banter — he computed that he, Mansell and Brundle had a combined age of '120 years' — Schumacher spoke. You couldn't miss that he was struggling to get the pitch right; he felt towards the occasion as he might have felt for the mouth of any corner, conscious of what a bump might bring. The interviewer said that presumably he would not have wished to see the Championship decided in this way. I set down Schumacher's response verbatim, and as it was spoken, because it ought to be so. I've only added a measure of interpretation in square brackets.

'Certainly. It was a great battle between me and Damon in the state of the race and I have to say he has done a really good job during it. We both didn't make mistakes and it was really, I would say, thrilling for you on the outside.

'I have to say I did make some comments this year about Damon that I didn't have the kind of respect for him that maybe I had for somebody else [Senna, no doubt], but I have to admit that I was wrong. What he has done in the last two races in particular — and what he did before — has been a fantastic job. He has been a great rival and I must say sorry for what I maybe said. I'd like to congratulate him.

'Nevertheless the feeling about the Championship, winning the Championship . . . I nearly won it earlier this year and then I got banned for a couple of races and couldn't continue. I lost a lot of points so I thought, "Now it's going to be very, very tough and difficult to make this Championship up again." Just sitting here now having won it, it's a dream, it's, it's . . .

'The emotions in me, I mean Nigel can talk about this as well. You can't really bring it outside. I have them here but I can't express them . . .'

Mansell: 'It'll get better . . .'

'It will get better? I must also say that this year our team has done a really, really good job. With the package we had available we really squeezed out a hundred per cent. There was nothing left. As you saw, it got more and more difficult towards the end of the season and I'd like to thank those people.

'I have something special to say about this whole season. The season started quite well, I would say, in Brazil. Aida was a good race and then we came up to Imola. What happened there is just a . . . if I talked about nightmares before that [I didn't know about nightmares]. All of us know what kind of feelings we had to make, particularly about Ayrton but as well for Roland, and for Karl after his crash at Monte Carlo.

'To me it was always clear that I was not going to win the Championship, and it was Ayrton who was going to win the Championship. But he hasn't been here for the last races and I'd like to take this Championship and give it to him. He is the driver who should have won it. He was the best driver, he had the best car and those are my feelings about him. It was difficult at the time to show those feelings because I am not somebody who likes to show their feelings to the outside world, but I always thought about it and it's the right time now to do something: to give something which I achieved — and he should have achieved — to him.'

Then it was time, high time, to put a Crocodile Dundee hat on and go dancing amidst a happy throng of a party, undulating, smiling, undulating, smiling. And he did, and he did, to celebrate as it is politic and desirable to do, and to remember and never to forget. Next day, composure regained, he was pressed about the crash of '94 and insisted in his quiet, methodical way, 'I was still in front of Damon. I drove over his front wheel. It was still my corner . . .'

• APPENDIX •

Michael Schumacher's Career Statistics

NC = Non-championship; DIS = disqualified; DNF = did not finish; DNS = did not start; P = pole; FL = fastest lap; R = retired; SWC = Sportscar World Championship.

The karting years

1984	German Junior Championship	1

1985	German Junior Championship	1
	Junior World Championship (Le Mans)	2

1986	German Senior Championship	
	(9th, Garching; 4th, Odenwald; 1st Utersen; 2nd Hagen)	3
	Munkolm 79 pts, Rabe 49, Schumacher 47	
	European Championship North Zone (Gothenburg)	2
	European Championship Final (Oppenrod)	3

1987	German Senior Championship	
	(1st Kerpen; 3rd Geesthacht; 1st Fassberg;	
	1st Wittenborn; 3rd Fulda; 1st Oppenrod;	
	1st Burg-Brueggen; 2nd Walldorf)	1

Schumacher 127 pts, Hantscher 112, Gruhn 68				
European Championship North Zone (Genk)				2
European Championship Final (Gothenburg)				1
S African Grand Prix (Kyalami)				2

The car years

1988

(FK = Formula Koenig; EF = Formula Ford 1600 Euroseries;
GF = German Formula Ford 1600)

Date	Series	Circuit	Car	Result
24 Apr	FK	Hockenheim	Fiat	1
8 May	FK	Nurburgring	Fiat	1
22 May	FK	Zolder	Fiat	2
12 June	FK	Hamburg	Fiat	1
24 July	FK	Luxemburg	Fiat	1
31 July	EF	Osterreichring	Van Diemen	2
7 Aug	EF	Knutstorp	Van Diemen	2
21 Aug	FK	Siegerland	Fiat	1
11 Sept	FK	Zolder	Fiat	1
	EF	Zolder	Van Diemen	P/R
18 Sept	EF	Zandvoort	Van Diemen	1
2 Oct	FK	Hockenheim	Fiat	1/FL
16 Oct	FK	Hockenheim	Fiat	1
23 Oct	FK	Nurburgring	Fiat	1/P
30 Oct	FF1600 Festival	Brands	Van Diemen	R

FK: Schumacher 192, G Hutter 131.5, H Schwitalla 122.5,
EF: M Salo 80, Schumacher 50, M Wagner 45

1989 German Formula 3

Date		Circuit	Car	Result
18 Mar	NC	Hockenheim	Reynard 893 VW	2/FL
2 Apr	NC	Hockenheim	Reynard 893 VW	1
16 Apr		Hockenheim	Reynard 893 VW	3
30 Apr		Nurburgring	Reynard 893 VW	3
28 May		Avus	Reynard 893 VW	3
11 June		Brunn	Reynard 893 VW	5
18 June		Zeltweg	Reynard 893 VW	1/P
2 July		Hockenheim	Reynard 893 VW	3
9 July		Wunstorf	Reynard 893 VW	12

29 July		Hockenheim	Reynard 893 VW	DNF
6 August		Diepholz	Reynard 893 VW	4
9 Sept		Nurburgring	Reynard 893 VW	5
24 Sept		Nurburgring	Reynard 893 VW	1/P
30 Sept		Hockenheim	Reynard 893 VW	3
26 Nov	F3 GP	Macau	Reynard-Speiss VW	R

Wendlinger 164, Frentzen 163, Schumacher 163

1990 German Formula 3

25 Mar	NC	Hockenheim	Reynard 390 VW	1
31 Mar		Zolder	Reynard 390 VW	DNF/P
7 Apr		Hockenheim	Reynard 390 VW	19/P
21 Apr		Nurburgring	Reynard 390 VW	5
5 May		Avus	Reynard 390 VW	1/FL
20 May	SWC	Silverstone	Mercedes C11	DNS
2 June		Wunstorf	Reynard 390 VW	1/P
30 June		Norisring	Reynard 390 VW	2
14 July		Zeltweg	Reynard 390 VW	1/P/FL
22 July	SWC	Dijon	Mercedes C11	2
4 Aug		Diepholz	Reynard 390 VW	1/FL
18 Aug		Nurburgring	Reynard 390 VW	1/P/FL
19 Aug	SWC	Nurburgring	Mercedes C11	2
1 Sept		Nurburgring	Reynard 390 Opel	4/P
7 Oct	SWC	Mexico	Mercedes C11	1/FL
13 Oct		Hockenheim	Reynard 390 VW	2
25 Nov	Int F3	Macau	Reynard-Spiess	1
2 Dec	Int F3	Fuji	Reynard-Spiess	1

German F3: Schumacher 148 pts, Rensing 117, Kaufmann 81, SWC: joint 5th, 21 pts

1991

14 Apr	SWC	Suzuka	Mercedes C291	R
5 May	SWC	Monza	Mercedes C291	R
19 May	SWC	Silverstone	Mercedes C291	2
22/23 June	SWC	Le Mans	Mercedes C11	5/FL
28 July	F3000	Sugo All-Japan	Ralt-Mugen	2
18 Aug	SWC	Nurburgring	Mercedes C11	R
25 Aug	Belgian GP	Spa	Jordan 191	R
8 Sept	Italian GP	Monza	Benetton B191	5

15 Sept	SWC	Magny-Cours	Mercedes C291	R
22 Sept	Portuguese GP	Estoril	Benetton B191	6
29 Sept	Spanish GP	Barcelona	Benetton B191	6
6 Oct	SWC	Mexico City	Mercedes C291	R
20 Oct	Japanese GP	Suzuka	Benetton B191	R
27 Oct	SWC	Autopolis	Mercedes C291	1
3 Nov	Australian GP	Adelaide	Benetton B191	R

SWC: joint 9th, 43 pts. Formula 1: joint 12th, 4 pts

1992

1 Mar	S African GP	Kyalami	Benetton B191B	4
22 Mar	Mexican GP	Mexico City	Benetton B191B	3
5 Apr	Brazilian GP	Interlagos	Benetton B191B	3
3 May	Spanish GP	Barcelona	Benetton B192	2
17 May	San Marino GP	Imola	Benetton B192	R
31 May	Monaco GP	Monte Carlo	Benetton B192	4
14 June	Canadian GP	Montreal	Benetton B192	2
5 July	French GP	Magny-Cours	Benetton B192	R
12 July	British GP	Silverstone	Benetton B192	4
26 July	German GP	Hockenheim	Benetton B192	3
16 Aug	Hungarian GP	Budapest	Benetton B192	R
30 Aug	Belgian GP	Spa	Benetton B192	1/FL
13 Sept	Italian GP	Monza	Benetton B192	3
27 Sept	Portuguese GP	Estoril	Benetton B192	7
25 Oct	Japanese GP	Suzuka	Benetton B192	R
8 Nov	Australian GP	Adelaide	Benetton B192	2/FL

Mansell 108 pts, Patrese 56, Schumacher 53, Senna 50

1993

14 Mar	S. African GP	Kyalami	Benetton B193A	R
28 Mar	Brazilian GP	Interlagos	Benetton B193A	3/FL
11 Apr	European GP	Donington	Benetton B193B	R
25 Apr	San Marino GP	Imola	Benetton B193B	2
9 May	Spanish GP	Barcelona	Benetton B193B	3/FL
23 May	Monaco GP	Monte Carlo	Benetton B193B	R
13 June	Canadian GP	Montreal	Benetton B193B	2/FL
4 July	French GP	Magny-Cours	Benetton B193B	3/FL
11 July	British GP	Silverstone	Benetton B193B	2

25 July	German GP	Hockenheim	Benetton B193B	2/FL
15 Aug	Hungarian GP	Budapest	Benetton B193B	R
29 Aug	Belgian GP	Spa	Benetton B193B	2
12 Sept	Italian GP	Monza	Benetton B193B	R
26 Sept	Portuguese GP	Estoril	Benetton B193B	1
24 Oct	Japanese GP	Suzuka	Benetton B193B	R
7 Nov	Australian GP	Adelaide	Benetton B193B	R

Prost 99 pts, Senna 73, Hill 69, Schumacher 52

1994 – World Champion

27 Mar	Brazilian GP	Interlagos	Benetton B194	1/FL
17 Apr	Pacific GP	Aida	Benetton B194	1/FL
1 May	San Marino GP	Imola	Benetton B194	1
15 May	Monaco GP	Monte Carlo	Benetton B194	1/P/FL
29 May	Spanish GP	Barcelona	Benetton B194	2/P/FL
12 June	Canadian GP	Montreal	Benetton B194	1/P/FL
3 July	French GP	Magny-Cours	Benetton B194	1
10 July	British GP	Silverstone	Benetton B194	(2) DIS
31 July	German GP	Hockenheim	Benetton B194	R
14 Aug	Hungarian GP	Budapest	Benetton B194	1/P/FL
28 Aug	Belgian GP	Spa	Benetton B194	(1) DIS

(Italian GP and Portuguese GP, did not take part: suspended.)

16 Oct	European GP	Jerez	Benetton B194	1/P/FL
6 Nov	Japanese GP	Suzuka	Benetton B194	2/P
13 Nov	Australian GP	Adelaide	Benetton B194	R/FL

Schumacher 92 pts, Hill 91, Berger 41

1995

26 Mar	Brazilian GP	Interlagos	Benetton B195	FL/1

(Disqualified, subsequently re-instated.)

9 Apr	Argentinian GP	Buenos Aires	Benetton B195	FL/3
30 Apr	San Marino GP	Imola	Benetton B195	P/R
14 May	Spanish GP	Barcelona	Benetton B195	P/1
28 May	Monaco GP	Monte Carlo	Benetton B195	1
11 June	Canadian GP	Montreal	Benetton B195	P/FL/5